"One of man's most noble emotions is patriotism—a deeply sincere and reverent love for his country. Unfortunately, patriotism is not innate, but must be taught to and learned by the individual.

"No greater example of selfless courage, achievement, and sacrifice can be found than that which permeates the sixty year chronicle of those patriots who have so greatly served our nation in the skies overhead. Realizing the inestimable value to be derived for future generations by permanently preserving the record of these flyers, the Air Force Museum Foundation has chosen to erect and present to the Government of the United States, for the benefit of all its people, an Air Force Museum facility worthy of the story to be told."

Eugene W. Kettering
    (1908–1969)
First Chairman of the Board, Air
Force Museum Foundation, Inc.

★ Contents

★ | *Foreword*

Americans have been fascinated with airplanes, new and old, since World War I. That interest accounts for our preeminence in aerospace from the dawn of flight to the first human footprints on the moon. As long as that interest continues, we shall hold our air and space leadership.

Here at the Air Force Museum, the oldest and largest of its kind in the world, is a reproduction of the army's first airplane and representatives of most types of U.S. military aircraft that have followed. Included are the planes that established most of the world's records of the last half century and also the fighters and bombers that enabled us to win all of our air wars.

As the United States moves toward its tricentennial, our people will reflect on our national heritage and keep its air power number one. American aviation leadership is a part of that proud heritage. The Air Force contributions to that heritage reside here in our Air Force Museum.

This book, with its crisp narrative and remarkable collection of historical photographs that take the reader on a chronological tour of military aviation in this country through two World Wars and outer space, including the first landing on the moon, makes our aviation heritage available to everyone. It's next best to visiting the Air Force Museum.

Ira C. Eaker
Lt. Gen., USAF (Ret.)

U.S. Air Force photo.

Retired Lt. Gen. Ira C. Eaker receives a Special Medal of Honor from Gen. Lew Allen, Jr., U.S. Air Force Chief of Staff. The pioneer aviator and World War II military commander was honored on December 17, 1979—the 76th Anniversary of Powered Flight.

THE AIR FORCE MUSEUM

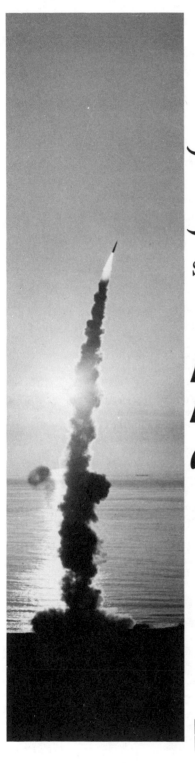

THE AIR FORCE MUSEUM

Sixth Revised Edition

By
Lt. Col. Nick P. Apple
and Lt. Col. Gene Gurney

 THE CENTRAL PRINTING CO., DAYTON, OHIO

The majority of the photographs credited to the
U.S. Air Force that show aircraft in and around the
U.S. Air Force Museum are the work of its long-
time photographer, Harry Elliott. The authors very
much appreciate his outstanding work.

Library of Congress Cataloging-in-Publication Data

Apple, Nick P
  The Air Force Museum.

  Includes index.
  1. United States.   Air Force Central Museum,
Wright-Patterson Air Force Base, Ohio.   2.   Aeronautics,
Military—History.   I. Gurney, Gene, joint author.
II.   Title.
UG623.3.U62D3832   1978   358.4′0074′017173   77-17895
ISBN 0-517-56296-0 (cloth)
      0-517-56297-9 (paper)

The Birth of the Air Force Museum

"There shall be wings. . . . If this accomplishment be not for me, 'tis for some other. . . ." These words were spoken more than four hundred years ago by Leonardo da Vinci. Today man has wings and they are displayed for the public at the United States Air Force Museum, internationally recognized as the world's oldest and largest military aviation museum. It is appropriately located near Dayton, Ohio at Wright-Patterson Air Force Base where the Wright brothers developed the first airplane and where they perfected their flying skills.

The Air Force Museum story is a moving one, an epic of men and machines, starting with ancient history and continuing through today. Man's first thoughts about flight, Leonardo's experiments with helicopters, kites and gliders, ballooning, and dirigibles are all displayed for visitors as they first enter the museum. They quickly meet the Wright brothers and continue with the flying crates of World War I, the exciting "first" flights of the 1920s and 1930s, the action of World War II, Korea, and Vietnam, and then step into the space age.

As a national museum of aviation history, it does not glorify war or dwell on the destructive aspects of combat. It illustrates through historic airplanes and authentic displays the development of aviation and the development of airpower, primarily as embodied in the United States Air Force. And the museum points out how military aviation has brought major advancements to civil aviation. Knowledge gained from the four years of the First World War played an important role in developing civil aviation for the next twenty years. The same was true of later years. For example, the Boeing 707 jet transport, the backbone of the commercial airline fleet, was developed from the Air Force's KC-135 tanker.

1

The Air Force Museum story is not static, as exhibits constantly are being added or enlarged, both indoors and out. Approximately six thousand of the forty-four thousand items in the museum's collection are currently on public view. Historic aircraft comprise the major displays, but they also include such things as clothing and diaries of flying aces, prisoner-of-war exhibits, Stumpy the homing pigeon, a German buzz bomb, and American military chapel display, and actual capsules from early space exploration. Also, aircraft from Germany, Japan, and the Soviet Union are on display. The museum is a virtual paradise for the aviation buff or the camera bug. More important, it is a place of interest for everyone, as attested to by the attendance figures of 1.5 million visitors annually.

Former Air Force crewmen who visit the museum often stand in silent tribute before the representative aircraft that carried them around the United States and over foreign lands. Oftentimes they can be overheard relating their experiences to friends or their children and grandchildren. Before they walk away, they nearly always reach over and touch the wing tip or propeller of the type airplane they flew many years before. That gesture is like a final farewell to a faithful and trusted comrade-in-arms.

In addition to the aircraft and other exhibits, famous people in world aviation history are depicted at the Air Force Museum. The visitor can find displays honoring such people as Octave Chanute, who built gliders as a first step toward a powered flying machine; Capt. Eddie Rickenbacker, the top American World War I ace; and all the other Air Force recipients of the Medal of Honor. Unexpected, perhaps, is the exhibit honoring musician Glenn Miller who, as a major, commanded the famous Army Air Forces Band during World War II. However, the Glenn Miller band was acclaimed as "the greatest morale builder" in Europe, second only to letters from home. The Air Force Museum tells the Glenn Miller story in a simple display which includes his original trombone (which was used by actor James Stewart in the Glenn Miller movie), his "fifty mission crush" hat, eyeglasses, and music case.

From its meager beginnings in 1923 in a corner of a hanger, the Air Force Museum has expanded into a $25 million facility constructed in 1970/71 and enlarged in 1975/76, in 1985/87, and again in 1989/91 on a 400-acre site. The area lies in the northwestern portion of the old Wright Field, between a runway and taxiway, and within three miles of Huffman Prairie where the Wright brothers developed the art of controlled flight in 1904 and 1905. Here they established a flying school and trained many of America's pioneer pilots. Today the area is a portion of Patterson Field which with Wright Field comprises Wright-Patterson Air Force Base. Wright Field is no less historic in its own right. Since its dedication in 1927, Wright Field has been known as an Air Force center for research and development. Numerous aircraft were tested and accepted here by the Air Force in the two decades before World War II.

Back in 1923, the first museum was located in Dayton at McCook Field, the Aeronautical Engineering Center established during World War I. The museum's mission called for the collection of technical intelligence related to American and foreign aircraft and equipment used in the previous war. It was moved to Wright Field in 1927 and occupied 1,500 square feet in a laboratory building. Then in 1935, the museum got its first real home, a $235,000 building provided by a federal works project. With a collection of about two thousand items, the new museum at Wright Field was opened to the public in 1936. The two-story WPA (Works Projects Administration) structure is still visible from the road near the railroad overpass as visitors approach the permanent museum from the north.

With the advent of World War II, Wright Field was closed to the public and the museum building converted to wartime office use. Museum property went into storage and remained there until long after that war. After the Allied victory over Germany and Japan, an engine overhaul building at Patterson Field was designated as the museum's new home. Curator Mark Sloan, who retired in 1972, began the search in 1946 for items for both the Air Force Museum and the National Air and Space Museum of the Smithsonian Institution. After eight years of acquiring and preparing items for display, the Air Force Museum opened in 1954 at its fourth location. But the 1954–1971 museum was from the beginning only a temporary home. It was not fireproof or air-conditioned, and it had supporting posts every sixteen feet in one direction and every fifty feet in the other. All of this made it unsuitable for properly displaying and protecting the museum's growing, priceless collection. By the early 1960s the building itself was outgrown, and there was little expansion room for the adjoining outdoor aircraft display area.

In 1960, a group of private citizens under the leadership of Dayton philanthropist Eugene W. Kettering chartered the Air Force Museum Foundation as a non-profit, tax-exempt organization. He brought together individuals from industrial, governmental, educational, and philanthropic organizations to form a board of directors for the foundation. Their objectives were to "foster and perpetuate the Air Force Museum by serving as a philanthropic corporation in the development and expansion of the museum facilities, and by receiving, holding, and administering gifts from persons, organizations, foundations, and philanthropies." In 1964

Guests arriving for special evening activities at the U.S. Air Force Museum have had this view of the modern facility since May 1991. The 500-seat IMAX Theater is contained within the structure to the left while the five-story atrium lobby is to the right. *U.S. Air Force photo.*

they launched a fund drive that eventually netted six million dollars, largely from Kettering, members of his family, and from local and national business and industry, organizations, private citizens, and from officers and airmen of the United States Air Force, including those on active duty, reservists, guardsmen, and veterans. Construction of the new museum started in April 1970; the museum was opened to the public in August 1971 and President Nixon dedicated it the following month. But Kettering did not live to see his project completed; he died in 1969.

This permanent museum structure is 766 feet long and follows the design of two aviation hangars joined by a "core" administrative section which has a winglike roof. Each of the hangars, or galleries, has an arched roof that reaches eighty feet above the ground. The interior width is 240 feet, or exactly twice the distance first flown by Orville Wright on December 17, 1903. More than 230,000 square feet of space is incorporated in the structure, including a total of 160,000 square feet of uninterrupted aircraft display space.

Approximately ninety aircraft and missiles are featured inside the 1971 structure. Early aviation history, Wright aircraft, those flown up to World War II, and associated memorabilia are displayed in the smaller of the two galleries, now known as the Early Years Gallery. Aircraft, weapons, space vehicles, and memorabilia of and since that war are exhibited in the larger or Air Power Gallery. More than forty aircraft and missiles initially were displayed outdoors. (To prevent further deterioration they were moved temporarily in 1977 across the field to two old hangers now designated the museum Annex.) The B-36 Peacemaker bomber was the first aircraft placed in the new quarters. With an wingspan of 230 feet, it had to be moved into position before the museum was completed. Its wing tips stretch almost from wall to wall, nearly twice the distance of man's first powered flight. Like the first Wright airplane, the B-36 also has propellers mounted behind the wing.

In the core area of the museum structure can be found a number of smaller displays, including the $500,000 Kettering collection of scale model planes, a portion of the Air Force art collection, pilot wings from around the world, emblems of major Air Force commands, winners of the Medal of Honor, the research division, the Air Force Museum Foundation gift shop, a restaurant, and administrative offices. A 500-seat auditorium is included for special presentations, movies, and meetings. The entire museum structure is air-conditioned and heated to provide visitor comfort and to help preserve the older fabrics, wooden aircraft, and related artifacts.

In 1971 the National Society of Professional Engineers presented a plaque to the Air Force Museum in recognition of its selection as one of the seven engineering wonders in Ohio. Museum exhibits, including World War II POW display and the unique display of aircraft spark plugs, have won national awards.

During 1975/76 a two-story addition was constructed in front of the core building at the cost of slightly more than $900,000 received from the Air Force Museum Foundation for the Air Force, and a contribution from the estate of Brig. Gen Erik H. Nelson, who died in 1970. He participated in 1924 in the first flight around the world. The addition contains a reception area on the ground floor, offices on the mezzanine, and an enlarged restaurant on the top level. It also affords a view of the outdoor missile park. Ground was broken in October 1985 for another addition, the Modern Flight Gallery, which was completed in December 1987 and officially opened in April 1988. This hangar-like structure measures nearly 800 feet by 200 feet and is located behind and parallel to the main museum building. Half of the $10.8 million cost was voted by the Congress and the remainder was raised by public donations through the foundation. With the Annex, 10.5 acres of exhibits then were under roof, making the U.S. Air Force Museum the largest in the world.

A much different addition was completed and dedicated in May 1991—a giant wide-screen theater. Work on this 500-seat IMAX Theater began shortly after the contract was awarded in October 1989. The $8 million project also includes an 80-foot-high dome glass atrium over a new lobby which serves as the architectural focal point of the entire museum complex. Aviation and space movies are featured in the IMAX Theater. Its six-story screen, sophisticated sound and tiered continental seating tend to bring viewers into the action being projected in front of them. An admission fee is charged to the theater, and proceeds are to help pay for further expansions at the museum.

The museum's staff also plans for the acquisition of other aircraft of historical importance. Orders are in with the federal government for a host of interesting airplanes, including the VC-137 in which Lyndon Johnson was sworn in as president. President Truman's VC-118 and President Eisenhower's VC-121E are already at the museum, as well as the latter's H-13J Sioux helicopter. Of course, most of the museum's aircraft are ones that have become surplus to Air Force use. Some have come through loans or trades with private individuals or other museums. Occasionally a museum friend will purchase a particular airplane and donate it to the Air Force. A number of World War II vintage aircraft have come from foreign nations. At least two have made their way to the museum through the circumstances of pilots defecting, one from Rumania with a Junkers Ju-88D-1 and another from North Korea with a MiG-15.

Another way of acquiring specific airplanes has been the research and evaluation of craft that crashed in remote areas years ago. The Museum's O-38 observation

More than 10-1/2 acres of exhibits are displayed under roof at the United States Air Force Museum. Its IMAX Theater and atrium lobby *(left)* were added in 1991 by the Air Force Museum Foundation, Inc., a philanthropic support organization established in 1960. *U.S. Air Force Photo.*

airplane lay in the Alaskan wilderness from 1941 to 1968 when it was recovered by helicopter and brought to the museum in pieces for restoration. A Japanese Zero, reclaimed from a South Pacific island, was retrieved from Australia and delivered to the museum for restoration. Often the airlift support is arranged by the Air Force Logistics Command at Wright-Patterson Air Force Base. When all else fails, the museum staff will construct a desired aircraft from original drawings, some authentic parts, and reproduced parts. The completion of a British Sopwith Camel of World War I fame was delayed somewhat in 1974 because its original French Clerget engine was not in operating condition. Such is the professional skill of the museum staff.

Nearly a year before the new museum was opened in 1971, more than thirty aircraft were towed approximately seven miles from the exhibit area at Patterson Field to Wright Field. Others were moved later. Highway signs and signal lights had to be removed in some areas. The Air Force's only remaining XB-70 experimental bomber was one of those to make the circuitous trip. Men of the Air Force Logistics Command had to strip the supersonic jet of her six engines and ten tons of equipment to reduce her weight to the stress limit of a highway bridge along the route. The engines have since been reinstalled.

When President Nixon flew to Wright-Patterson Air Force Base aboard his *Spirit of '76* to dedicate the facility officially on September 3, 1971, he told of Orville Wright's taking his father for a flight over Huffman Prairie and of the elder Wright's speaking these words: "Higher, higher, higher." The President continued: "That was the spirit of American aviation. That is the spirit of the American Air Force. . . . And let that spirit, higher and higher, always be the spirit of the United States of America." The words were spoken in the Air Power Gallery against the backdrop of the nose of the B-36 Peacemaker and before a crowd of twelve thousand spectators, including those hearing the address via loudspeakers outdoors. Frank G. Anger, president of the Air Force Museum Foundation, earlier in the program had presented the museum building to Secretary of the Air Force Robert C. Seamans, Jr., who accepted it on behalf of the Air Force.

Although the museum is operated and maintained by the Air Force, the private Air Force Museum Foundation continues its support. Through its office at the museum, the foundation operates the museum gift shop and IMAX Theater, contracts for the operation of the restaurant, raises funds, and generally assists wherever and whenever possible and practicable. When government resources were not available, for example, the foundation purchased wheelchairs and picnic tables for visitors and obtained a special display case and protection system for the museum's moon rock. Contributions to the foundation are tax deductible. In January 1978, the foundation initiated a membership program, "Friends of the United States Air Force Museum," to draw together aviation enthusiasts who are interested in the activities of the museum and in furthering its aims. Volunteer assistance is also given the museum by members of the Wright-Patterson Air Force Base Officers' Wives Club who conduct tours for youngsters on a prescheduled basis and by many other volunteers throughout the museum.

One of the objectives of the official museum of the Air Force is to serve as an educational tool for teaching young people about aviation. Secretary Seamans in 1971 perhaps best summarized the goal of the museum in these words: "The new Air Force Museum will serve as a tribute to all Americans who have contributed so much to the field of aviation. It will also serve as an inspiration to future generations of Americans to increase their knowledge and awareness of the United States Air Force and the history of flight." As Ohio's top public attraction since his remarks were made, the U.S. Air Force Museum continues to fulfill its mission with international acclaim.

The Air Force Museum is open to the public without parking or admission charge seven days a week from 9:00 A.M. to 5:00 P.M. It is closed only on Thanksgiving, Christmas, and New Year's Day. Visitors should exit Ohio Route 4 at Harshman Road about five miles northeast of Dayton. Signs indicate the directions to the museum. Use Exit 58 (Needmore Road) at I-75 in Dayton and I-70 and Route 4 at Exit 13. Photographing Air Force Museum exhibits is encouraged. Flash equipment or tripods for time exposures will be required for indoor pictures. Facilities are available for persons with disabilities. Pets are not permitted. Other areas of Wright-Patterson Air Force Base, excluding the temporary museum Annex, are restricted and closed to the public. For current information, telephone (513) 255-3286 or write the U.S. Air Force Museum, Wright-Patterson AFB, Ohio 45433-6518.

Overlooking old Huffman Prairie, where Orville and Wilbur Wright perfected their flying techniques, is this monument commemorating their achievements as scientists and inventors. Appropriately, this rise in the landscape, between Wright and Patterson Fields, is called Wright Brothers Hill.

Missiles dominate the scene in front of the museum. Visitors are encouraged to bring their cameras. Wright Brothers Hill is in the left, background.

Famous visitors frequently visit the museum, among them the Goodyear blimp *(right of center)*. President Truman's airplane the *Independence* is visible *(on the left)* between the Atlas and shorter Thor missiles. Free parking and a picnic area are located in the right background.

Patriotic bunting decorated the museum on September 3, 1971, when the new $6 million facility was dedicated by President Nixon. It also rained that day, but twelve thousand people braved the weather to attend the ceremony. The central portion was expanded in 1975/76 at a cost of nearly $1 million. *U. S. Air Force photo.*

UNITED STATES AIR FORCE MUSEUM

SINCE THE WRIGHT BROTHERS' FIRST FLIGHT, THE HISTORY OF AVIATION HAS BEEN MARKED BY THE COURAGE AND CONSUMING DESIRE FOR KNOWLEDGE WHICH HAVE ENABLED MANKIND IN A RELATIVELY FEW YEARS TO LEAVE THE EARTH AND BEGIN THE EXPLORATION OF SPACE.

THIS MUSEUM WHICH IS MEANT TO PRESERVE THE HERITAGE OF MILITARY AVIATION, WAS BUILT BY THE AIR FORCE MUSEUM FOUNDATION UNDER THE LEADERSHIP OF EUGENE W. KETTERING AND WITH THE GENEROUS VOLUNTARY SUPPORT OF U.S. AIR FORCE PERSONNEL, INDUSTRY, AND INTERESTED INDIVIDUALS.

ON BEHALF OF A GRATEFUL NATION, I JOIN IN DEDICATING THIS AIR FORCE MUSEUM TO THE AMERICAN PEOPLE AND TO THE THOUSANDS OF AIRMEN WHOSE PIONEERING SPIRIT, DEVOTION TO DUTY AND LOVE OF FLYING HAVE CONTRIBUTED SO MUCH TO OUR PROGRESS IN THE AIR AND TO OUR HAPPINESS ON THE EARTH.

RICHARD NIXON

SEPTEMBER 3, 1971

This plaque hangs on the outside wall near the museum entrance.

9

General Jack G. Merrell, commander of the Air Force Logistics Command, opened the official ceremonies with President Richard Nixon seated directly in front of the B-36 Peacemaker. Key platform guests included Mr. Frank G. Anger, president of the Air Force Museum Foundation; Ohio Governor John J. Gilligan; and Mr. Robert S. Oelman, chairman of the board, Air Force Museum Foundation. *U.S. Air Force photo.*

President Nixon accepted the museum from the Air Force Museum Foundation, Inc., on behalf of the American people. He called on the nation to continue leading the world in aviation. *U.S. Air Force photos.*

Museum dedication guests had an opportunity to view the older airplanes in the Early Years Gallery which has since been partitioned into a maze that directs visitors on a chronological walk through aviation history. *U.S. Air Force photo.*

Secretary of the Air Force Robert C. Seamans, Jr., presented a model of the museum to Mrs. Eugene W. Kettering, whose late husband spearheaded the campaign for the new facility. Gen. and Mrs. Jack G. Merrell look on. The general commanded the Air Force Logistics Command which provides much of the support for the museum. *U.S. Air Force photo.*

This metal plaque is a full-scale reproduction of the *Dayton Daily News* special edition which was distributed at Wright-Patterson Air Force Base when the museum was dedicated by President Nixon. It includes an article referring to Dayton, Ohio, as the birthplace of aviation. It also includes a reference to a future era of unmanned military aircraft called "remotely piloted vehicles."

The growth of the Air Force Museum from its meager beginnings in a corner of a hangar in 1923 until today is shown in this display.

A corner of this McCook Field hangar housed the first museum from 1923 until 1927. Originally the museum was called the Engineering Division Museum. *U.S. Air Force photo.*

Some of the World War I airplanes displayed at the McCook Field museum. Wings were removed so that more planes could be housed in the limited space available. *U.S. Air Force photo.*

In 1927 the museum's artifacts were moved to the new Wright Field. Since no museum building was available there, engines, propellers, other items of aeronautical equipment, and a few airplanes were exhibited in the back of this laboratory building until another move in 1935. In 1932 the collection was renamed the Army Aeronautical Museum. *U.S. Air Force photo.*

12

A special museum building was constructed at Wright Field, and in June 1935 the museum moved into it. Unfortunately, the world situation in 1940 forced the closing of the museum so the building could be used for offices by the rapidly expanding United States Army Air Corps. Its artifacts were stored wherever space was available for the duration of World War II. *U.S. Air Force photo.*

An interior view of the 1935 building showing some museum displays. A need for an aviation museum in the United States had been long recognized. Pioneers professed that many hours of needless engineering research might be saved if examples of what had already been accomplished were readily available. *U.S. Air Force photo.*

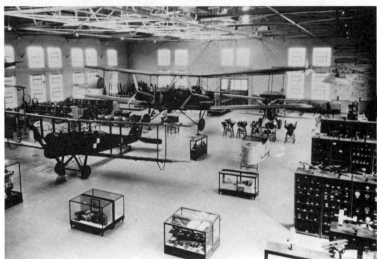

Following World War II an engine overhaul building at Patterson Field was obtained for the museum, and on January 2, 1948, the Air Force Technical Museum was officially established as the successor to the Army Aeronautical Museum. Originally the Technical Museum displayed only technical items such as engines and cameras, but in 1954 it began to acquire full-size airplanes for public exhibit. Two years later it officially became the Air Force Museum. *U.S. Air Force photo.*

The fourth museum looked like this in its final years. During the Christmas holidays the Atlas missile was decorated to resemble a giant Santa Claus. Many of the airplanes which were formerly parked outdoors, including the giant B-36, are now displayed indoors. *U.S. Air Force photos.*

Since World War II, the following men have served as directors of the Air Force Museum:

Mr. Mark Sloan	1946–56
Col. John F. Wadman	1957–58
Maj. Robert L. Bryant, Jr.	1958–62
Lt. Col. Kimbrough S. Brown	1962–63
Capt. Burdette E. Townsend	1963–64
Col. William F. Curry	1964–67
Col. Joseph D. Hornsby	1967–70
Col. Bernie S. Bass	1970–76
Col. Richard L. Uppstrom	1976–

Some of the items on exhibit during the 1950s. Numerous pillars and a relatively low ceiling in the building often interfered with properly displaying the exhibits. *U.S. Air Force photo.*

This B-25 bomber led a B-24 and a string of other aircraft along Route 444 from the old museum at Patterson Field, past Wright Brothers Hill, to their new home at Wright Field. Several governmental agencies cooperated in this unusual "flight." *U.S. Air Force photo.*

Wing tips had to be temporarily removed from this B-24D Liberator so that it could be towed to the new museum. Thirty airplanes were moved on two consecutive weekends. *U.S. Air Force photo.*

The direct route to the new museum would have been via the road to the left, but a narrow railroad bridge necessitated a longer route freer of obstructions. *U.S. Air Force photo.*

Before the XB-70 could be moved, ten tons of equipment and six jet engines had to be stripped from the Valkyrie so that it would not damage the bridge. Traffic signals had to be removed from some intersections to permit the aircraft to pass through. Wright Brothers Hill is in the background. *U.S. Air Force photo.*

After its seven-mile journey to the new museum, the once-secret XB-70 invited visitors to inspect it and the museum closely. Aircraft, such as the KC-135 tanker, regularly pass overhead at a low, but safe altitude. They provide an added dimension to the static airplanes on display. The XB-70 was moved into the Modern Flight Gallery after it was completed in 1987.

15

Six-inch-diameter pins fasten the parabolic museum roof to concrete piers which weigh three-and-a-half tons each. President Truman's VC-118 airplane is also pictured. It has been repainted and moved into the Annex.

Contractors' plaque.

Beside the staircase leading to the second floor is this plaque, a gift from plasterers who worked on the museum construction. It was made on their own time and presented as a memento of their interest in the museum.

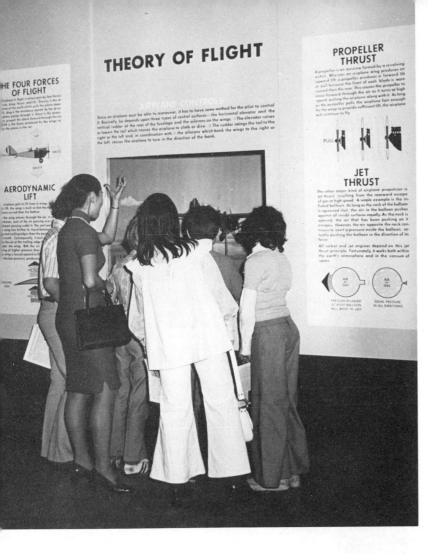

Groups of school-age children are taken on conducted tours by volunteers from the Wright-Patterson Air Force Base Officer's Wives Club. The tours are offered only during the school year. Arrangements must be made in advance, either by letter or by telephoning the museum. *U.S. Air Force photo.*

Girl Scouts on an information Discovery Tour peer into the cockpit of a North American T-6 trainer in the Early Years Gallery. Such free tours are arranged in advance through the museum's education officer. *U.S. Air Force photo.*

Aviation-related souvenirs, gifts, and models of all sizes and descriptions are available at the gift shop operated by the Air Force Museum Foundation. The museum bookstore, located along a facing wall, is the largest aviation bookstore in any aviation museum in the United States. Profits from these shops and a 300-seat restaurant upstairs help the foundation purchase needed items which the museum is unable to obtain through government sources.

U.S. Air Force photo.

The foundation's Friends of the Air Force Museum program also assists in the development of museum facilities through a membership program. Individual benefits from an annual $15 fee include a membership card, certificate, calendar, museum aircraft booklet, newsletter, discounts on books and gifts (both over the counter and via mail order), and notification and invitations to special museum events. Higher category individual annual memberships are also available and carry increased benefits to the members. *U.S. Air Force photo.*

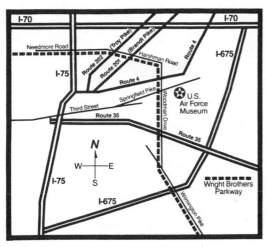

Main highways in Ohio lead visitors to the Air Force Museum and its year-round "greeter", the Rockwell B-1A bomber. Downtown Dayton is located near the I-75/Route 35 interchange.

Some fifty aircraft are among the "eagles" that rest in the Modern Flight Gallery *(rear hanger-like structure in above photograph)*. A North American F-86D Sabre fighter and a Douglas C-124C Globemaster II transport are shown.

The North American XB-70 Valkyrie dominates the northern end of the Modern Flight Gallery. In the foreground are a Martin X-24B and a Douglas X-3 Stilleto. All three were flown in experimental projects.

19

Larger aircraft dominate the Outdoor Air Park, including the Lockheed EC-121D Constellation *(left)* and the Boeing NKC-135A airborne laser laboratory *(tail, right)*. In the distance, at the nose of the former, can be seen a likeness of the Wright brothers on the museum Annex. A number of airplanes have been displayed there since 1977.

A Schweitzer TG-3A training glider from World War II appears to soar over this small portion of the Early Years Gallery at the U.S. Air Force Museum. Coming up on its right wing is a North American BT-14 trainer and below is a Ryan PT-22 Recruit. This area focuses on training programs and aircraft that prepared American men and women for WW II. *U.S. Air Force photo.*

Convair built this B-36A Peacemaker, which dominates the Air Power Gallery. The exhibition area includes World War II displays beyond the nose of the B-36, Korean War displays in front of its wing, Vietnam War displays under and behind its tail, and the Space Gallery off of its left wing. *U.S. Air Force photo.*

★ 2 | *Early Aviation History*

Man's early concerns about aerial flight and his first attempts to slip the bonds of earth are portrayed at the Air Force Museum in models, sketches, photographs, and words. In this prologue to flight are presented the basic origins of man's eventual conquest of air and space. The history of flight begins with a representation of a bas-relief stone sculpture of Ashur, the winged deity who was venerated by the Assyrians hundreds of years before Christ. The history progresses quickly and chronologically to the world's first powered, sustained, and controlled heavier-than-air flight on December 17, 1903, at Kitty Hawk, North Carolina. Few people of the day recognized the revolutionary implications of that flight by Orville Wright. The world as they knew it has been reduced in scope because of that flight.

Understandably, the Air Force Museum devotes significant attention to the Wright brothers and their accomplishments. A few scraps of wood and fabric from the original 1903 Flyer are displayed, as well as original propellers and a bicycle from the Wright Cycle Company. More important, there is also a full-scale reproduction of the Wright 1909 Military Flyer (the first United States military airplane) and an original Wright 1911 Modified "B" Flyer.

Displays on the walls around these two air machines illustrate achievements in the development of aircraft by both the Wrights and the aviation wing of the Army. The latter had been established on August 1, 1907, by the War Department as the Aeronautical Division of the Office of the Chief Signal Officer of the Army. Command of what was to become the United States Air Force was given to Charles deForrest Chandler, who was described as "a dashing young captain with a venturesome spirit." He was ordered to take charge of "all matters pertaining to

21

military ballooning, air machines, and all kindred subjects." Two enlisted men and a civilian clerk were assigned to his staff.

In 1910, the Aeronautical Division had grown to fourteen men, including three flying officers. Two of them were later reassigned, so it fell to Lt. Benjamin D. Foulois to accept the first military airplane from the Wright brothers. Along with this responsibility, he was told to "assemble this flying machine and teach yourself to fly." With the aid of correspondence lessons from the Wright brothers, he did. One year later, Foulois and Chandler were joined by Lt. Henry "Hap" Arnold, who was to become the first General of the Air Force.

Early flyers, military and civilian, seemed bound together in a fraternity accepting a common challenge. Leaving the comfortable earth for the alien element of the skies demanded a blend of courage, curiosity, dedication, and daring. They played a dangerous game and accepted the consequences of losing. When Orville Wright conducted tests for the War Department in September 1908, Lt. Thomas E. Selfridge was his passenger. In the crash that ended these tests, Lieutenant Selfridge was fatally injured. He thus became the first to die as the result of an airplane accident. He had also been the first military man to fly an airplane alone. As fate would have it, he paid the price that airmen have faced since they first ventured off the ground.

In spite of dynamic personalities and leadership, however, the nation's love affair at this time was with the automobile and not with the airplane. The nation that gave birth to the airplane was following a course that would have us entering World War I with a twelfth-rate air arm. As World War I developed in Europe, the airplane was still considered a toy by most military men in America. A few realists, struggling against skeptics and inertia, developed the fledgling air force as best they could. These efforts, too, are presented to museum visitors as they wend their way through the exhibition maze in the Early Years Gallery to the end of the first major section of the museum.

Man's earliest dreams of flight welcome visitors to the Air Force Museum. Khensu, the upright creature with four wings, was the Egyptian Navigator of the Skies about 1000 B.C. To the left of the large sign is Ashur (not seen), the Assyrian winged deity.

Ashur and Khensu.

This prologue-to-flight section stirs the imagination of museum visitors. Flights attributed to mythology and actual flights in balloons and strange contraptions led to the Wright brothers' breathtaking flight at Kitty Hawk.

To achieve powered flight man first had to solve the problems of control and aerodynamic lift while developing a satisfactory lightweight engine. It required a hundred years of effort by many air-minded men before the Wright brothers first demonstrated powered, controlled, and sustained flight.

A bronze sculpture of Daedalus and his son Icarus hangs as a mute reminder that even the early Greeks were interested in flight. According to the myth, Daedalus and his son Icarus fashioned wings of wax and feathers. Icarus disobeyed his father's warning, flew too close to the sun, and fell to his death. The sculpture depicts Daedalus bearing up his dead son.

A very early pioneer in the study of flight was Leonardo da Vinci, who made this helicopter drawing in about 1500. Ridiculed about his concern with flight, Leonardo took to writing in code: the left-handed artist wrote backwards.

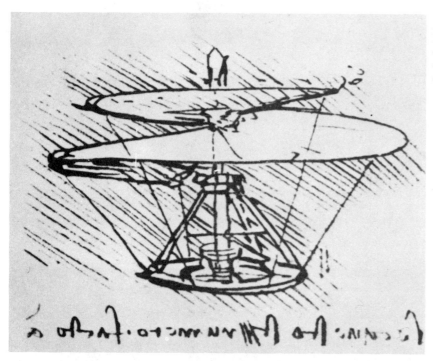

Leonardo's early helicopter drawing has been transformed by museum staff members into an animated model—one of the more popular displays with the younger visitors. Push a button and the contraption revolves within its plexiglas case.

The Montgolfier balloon lifted man in his first aerial flight on November 21, 1783, when Jean-François Pilâtre de Rozier and the Marquis d'Arlandes went aloft for a flight which lasted approximately twenty-five minutes and covered more than five miles across Paris. The two daring fliers alternately fed straw and wool to the fire which was suspended in a grate beneath the open end of the balloon. They watched closely to see that sparks did not ignite the flimsy linen-and-paper balloon overhead.

Military ballooning in the United States began early in the Civil War. Best known of the aeronauts was Thaddeus S. C. Lowe. He and others made numerous aerial observations during the first two years of the war. At one time there were seven balloons in service with the Union Army. The South had at least three balloons in service. Both sides suspended balloon operations in 1863.

Correspondence from Abraham Lincoln and a telegram concerning ballooning during the Civil War period. The telegram is signed T. S. C. Lowe, "Chief Aeronaut, U.S.A."

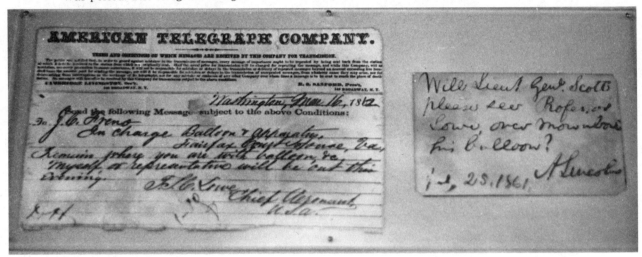

After the Civil War, there was no further military ballooning in the U.S. until 1892 when a balloon section was established within the Signal Corps. When war broke out in 1898, the Army's "air arm" consisted of one hand-sewn balloon. Despite incredible difficulties, Lt. Col. Joseph Maxfield succeeded in getting the balloon to Cuba where several ascents were made, including one in preparation for the famous charge up San Juan Hill. In 1899, the balloon detachment was disbanded and military aeronautics faded until 1907.

From the beginning, the usefulness of the balloon depended upon giving it "dirigibility" or directional control. This first demonstration flight of a Zeppelin occurred July 2, 1900.

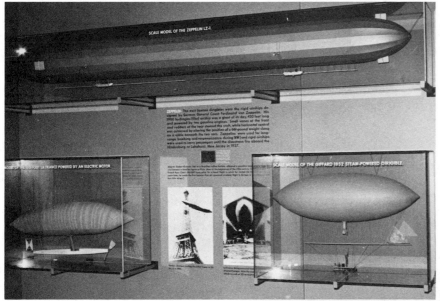

Three scale-model dirigibles are pictured in this display. At the top is the 420-foot German Zeppelin LZ-1, which flew in 1900. Left is the La France of 1884 and right the Giffard 1852 steam-powered dirigible.

Man's early attempts at flight included experiments with elaborate kites and wings.

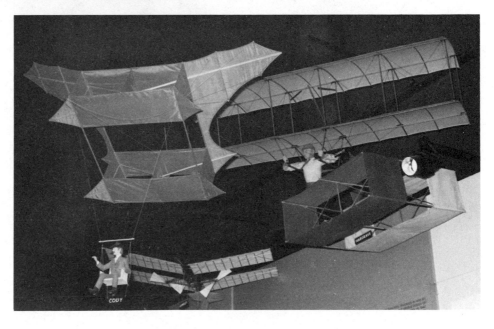

Otto Lilienthal was the greatest of the glider experimenters. He built his first glider in 1891 and within the next five years this brilliant German made more than two thousand glides. He was fatally injured in a gliding accident in 1896.

Sir Hiram Maxim, an American-born inventor, tested his giant steam-powered flying machine in 1894 on a half-mile track fitted with guard rails to prevent the craft from rising more than a few inches. But the machine broke through the rails, and Maxim stopped the engines, as well as further flying. He noted: "Propulsion and lifting are solved problems; the rest is a mere matter of time." Maxim made no mention of the third requirement of successful flight, proper control.

Octave Chanute. A successful civil engineer, Chanute applied his knowledge of bridge building to the design of gliders. Published in 1894, his classic volume *Progress in Flying Machines* brought together in one book a history of man's attempts to fly. No less important to aviation history was Chanute's role as friend and advisor to the Wright Brothers. Above is a model of Chanute's 1896 biplane glider, his most successful design.

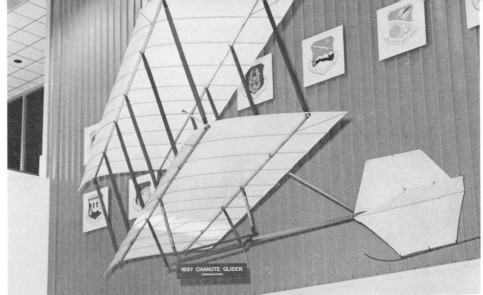

Charles Manly (left) and Samuel Pierpont Langley.

Langley's "aerodrome" prior to falling into the river.

Langley-type propeller

SAMUEL PIERPONT LANGLEY

An astronomer and Secretary of the Smithsonian Institution, Langley in 1896 flew a steam-driven airplane model three-fourths of a mile and in 1898 received a Congressional grant of $50,000 for further development. Convinced now that a gasoline engine offered more promise than steam, he and his gifted assistant, Charles M. Manly, designed and built a revolutionary aircraft powered by a 125 lb. 53 hp. gasoline engine. On October 7, 1903, Manly attempted to fly from the deck of a houseboat on the Potomac River, but the airplane apparently fouled some portion of the catapult mechanism and tumbled into the river. Manly tried again on December 8 and again the attempt failed. These failures, plus the cruel jeers of the newspapers and cynics, crushed Langley's spirit and he retired. Nine days later, as the world continued to jeer, the Wrights flew on a bleak beach in North Carolina.

1897 CHANUTE GLIDER

Octave Chanute was already a successful American civil engineer in his 60s when he first became fascinated by aviation. In 1894, his studies led him to publish a compilation of early aviation knowledge and history, _Progress in Flying Machines_ (republished in 1976). In addition to his significant contribution to aviation as a collector of aeronautical data, in 1895 he began designing and building gliders. These ranged from one using six tiers of wings to the successful biplane design which this reproduction represents. Mr. Chanute was aided by Mr. Augustus M. Herring, a civil and mechanical engineer, and Mr. William Avery, both of whom acted as pilot in various experimental and demonstration flights. Some of the gliders which Chanute designed and tested had either moveable wings or tail control surfaces; however each also relied on the pilot's body movements for proper equilibrium control. During the Wright Brothers' early experiments with gliders beginning in 1900, Chanute offered them encouragement and advice based on his own observations.

This reproduction represents Chanute's 1897 glider which was flown by Mr. William Avery 84 times at the St. Louis World's Fair in 1904. The craft was built in Chanute, Kansas by Mr. Johnny L. Litchenburg, using materials and construction methods similar to those employed in the fabrication of the original glider. Spruce and mahogany were used extensively in the original and the reproduction, as was brazing to join various metal components. One departure from the original techniques was the use of dacron rather than silk as the wing covering for greater resistance to deterioration through age while on display.

The glider was donated to the United States Air Force Museum by Octave Chanute's great-grandson, Mr. Octave A. Chanute, Director of the Historical Aircraft Research and Development Company of Denver, Col. It was jointly dedicated to the United States Air Force and the Chanute Technical Training Center in 1978.

After several experiments with steam-driven aircraft models, Samuel Pierpont Langley finally turned to the gasoline engine.

A wall display shows events leading up to the invention of the Wright brothers' gasoline-powered flying machine. Top right in the large display board is their Wright Cycle Company. Lower right is their first glider being flown as a kite. Closeups from the big board are included here. In 1901 and 1902 they developed and tested over fifty airfoil sections in a homemade wind tunnel and on a modified bicycle. In 1903 there was a photographer on hand to record their magnificent achievement.

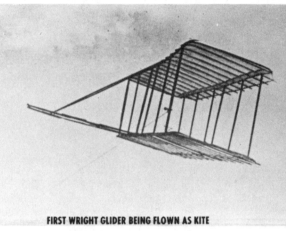

FIRST WRIGHT GLIDER BEING FLOWN AS KITE

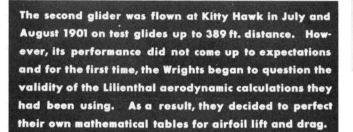

The second glider was flown at Kitty Hawk in July and August 1901 on test glides up to 389 ft. distance. However, its performance did not come up to expectations and for the first time, the Wrights began to question the validity of the Lilienthal aerodynamic calculations they had been using. As a result, they decided to perfect their own mathematical tables for airfoil lift and drag.

Third glider fitted with twin controllable rudders.

1903 AIRPLANE ON LAUNCHING RAIL

END OF FIRST ATTEMPT AT POWERED FLIGHT, DECEMBER 14, 1903

In the summer of 1903, they built an airplane of 40' 4" span which incorporated all the aerodynamic knowledge they had learned. While their mechanic, Charlie Taylor, built a small, lightweight gasoline engine, they designed and built propellers, a significant feat in itself. On December 14, 1903, Wilbur attempted to fly the machine but he over-corrected the elevator control and the airplane crashed. Three days later, the machine had been repaired and Orville flew it successfully for the first time.

1903

Take-off of the 1903 Wright flyer on the world's first powered, sustained, and controlled heavier-than-air flight, December 17, 1903 at Kitty Hawk, North Carolina. Piloted by Orville Wright, the airplane remained aloft for 12 seconds and flew a distance of 120 feet.

Life-size busts of Orville (*left*) and Wilbur Wright (*right*) flank the large photograph of their first flight at Kitty Hawk, North Carolina, on December 17, 1903.

An exact reproduction of the Wright 1909 Military Flyer, this plane displays an original engine donated by Orville Wright. He is depicted seated on the right. On the left is Lt. Frank P. Lahm, one of the first men trained to fly by Wilbur Wright, who is shown standing. On his right is Lt. Benjamin D. Foulois, who learned to fly the plane via correspondence with the Wright brothers. Two other views are included here.

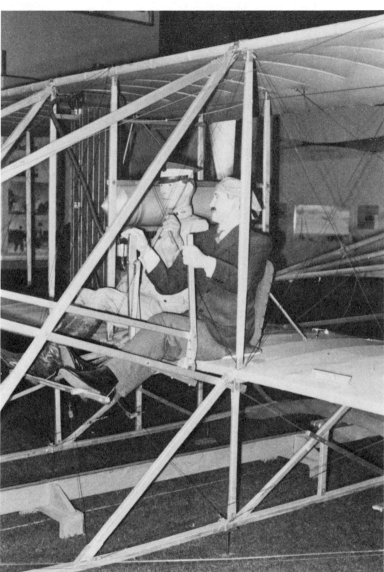

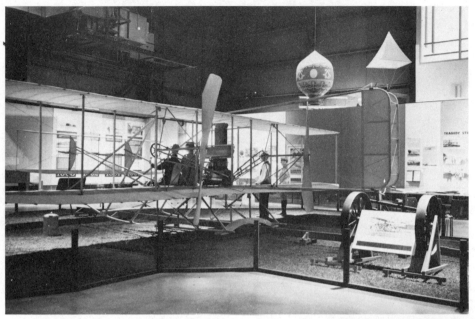

Rear view of the world's first military heavier-than-air flying machine, which had a maximum speed of forty-two miles per hour. The 1909 Military Flyer had skids similar to the X-15 which in 1966 set an unofficial world's speed record of 4,-520 miles per hour. Maneuvering wheels for the 1909 Flyer are in the foreground, also seen here separately in closeup.

Maneuvering wheels were placed under 1909 Flyer to permit the aircraft to be moved while on the ground; they were detached prior to flight.

Resting unobtrusively behind the 1909 Military Flyer is an original Wright brothers bicycle, purchased from the Wright Cycle Company in 1895.

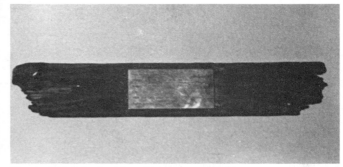

Piece of Wright brothers' hangar on Huffman Prairie given to Mr. E. N. Findley by Orville Wright in 1915. On September 20, 1904, Wilbur Wright made history's first full-circle airplane flight when he took off from Huffman Prairie and landed near the spot from which he had taken off.

During 1904 and 1905, the Wright brothers continued their research into the mysteries of flight over Huffman Prairie, now part of Wright-Patterson Air Force Base. On two occasions in 1905 they offered their invention to the U.S. Government. But their offers were rejected because few people actually believed they had invented a successful flying machine. This scene is at Simms Station, November 16, 1904.

Orville Wright prepares to take off in the 1908 Flyer with Maj. George O. Squier as his passenger on September 12, 1908. The front of the Wright Flyer is to the right.

Orville Wright circles Fort Myer, Virginia, during tests conducted in 1908 for the War Department. During these tests, he made the world's first flight of longer than one hour. *U.S. Air Force photo.*

Signal Corps No. 1, a Wright Flyer, is readied on the launching rail at College Park, Maryland (1909). A weight dropped from the tower in the background pulled a rope that catapulted the aircraft along the rail and into the air.

An original Wright 1911 Modified "B" Flyer shares the attention of museum visitors with wall exhibits. The 1911 Flyer is the first plane produced and sold in quantity by the Wright brothers. Displays on the walls concern the first bombs dropped from airplanes, first weapons fired from flying machines, and early U.S. aviation schools at College Park, Md.; Texas City, Tex.; San Diego, Calif.; and the Philippines.

This Wright 1911 Modified "B" Flyer is one of the Wrights' original planes and was last flown in the 1924 International Air Race in Dayton. Overhead is the 1909-type Blériot which was used for both air and ground pilot training. It achieved fame when designer Louis Blériot of France flew it to England, making it the first plane flown across the English Channel.

An eight-cylinder Rausenberger engine powered this 1911 Flyer to a top speed of 45 mph. With the engine placed off center, the weight of the pilot and passenger was relied upon to help balance the aircraft.

Shown are three wind tunnels, devices used for calibrating airspeed instruments and testing airfoils. The smallest tunnel is a replica of the one designed and built by the Wright brothers in 1901. It produced winds of from twenty-five to thirty-five miles per hour. This replica was constructed under the personal supervision of Orville Wright prior to World War II. The Orville Wright Wind Tunnel was designed by him in 1916 to conduct aerodynamic experiments during World War I at wind velocities greater than 160 miles per hour. The largest wind tunnel, seen here, was designed and built at McCook Field in Dayton in 1918. It has a twenty-four-blade fan sixty inches in diameter which achieved a maximum speed of 453 miles per hour at its fourteen-inch-diameter choke-throat test area.

The *Springfield* (Ohio) *Daily News* of May 30, 1912, ran an editorial drawing on the bottom of page one depicting an angel reaching out to receive Wilbur Wright on "His Last Flight." He had died of typhoid fever in Dayton. The newspaper also commemorated Memorial Day.

The *Dayton Daily News* of February 2, 1948, reported that "Civic life in Dayton came to virtual standstill Monday afternoon as Dayton paused to honor Orville Wright." A related headline called Orville a "Simple Man of Genius."

The first Gordon Bennett Balloon Trophy Race was won in 1906 by Lt. Frank P. Lahm and Maj. Henry B. Hersey when they traveled 402 miles across France in a free balloon. The first trophy, permanently awarded to Belgium in 1924, was donated in 1906 by James Gordon Bennett, an American newspaper publisher. The United States was awarded permanent possession of this second trophy in 1928 as a result of winning it for a third successive year when Capt. William E. Kepner and Lt. William Eareckson flew 460.9 miles in a free balloon from Detroit. It was donated by the Aero Club of Belgium.

Corporal Edward Ward, the first enlisted man to be assigned aviation duties in the Signal Corps, and other members of the balloon detachment, October, 1907. Early in 1907, the U.S. Army had become interested in ballooning and purchased two hydrogen balloons. One of these made a flight from Washington, D.C. to Harrisburg, Penna., on June 4, 1907. The Army observer on this flight was Capt. Charles deForest Chandler. Ballooning activities increased significantly during the following months as Army personnel gained aeronautical experience. Ward is in the center, seated.

40

During the 1910–1911 period, the Signal Corps had so few airplanes that it adopted a policy of granting its pilots necessary leave from duty to fly manufacturers' airplanes at civilian flying meets. At one such meet sponsored by the Aero Club of America on September 26, 1911, at the Nassau Boulevard Aerodrome on Long Island, Lt. Thomas Dewitt Milling, seen here, set a world endurance record of 1 hour 54 minutes 42.6 seconds with two passengers, for which he was awarded the Rodman Wanamaker Endurance Trophy. Milling, together with Lt. H. H. Arnold, was taught to fly in May 1911 at the Wright Company's flying school at Huffman Prairie, now part of Wright-Patterson Air Force Base.

America's first military aircraft engine, the Curtiss four-cylinder water-cooled engine, was used in the 1908 Signal Corps Dirigible No. 1. Developing about twenty-five horsepower, it drove a tubular steel shaft twenty-two feet long on which was mounted a wooden propeller designed by Lt. Thomas E. Selfridge. In the official speed trial the Baldwin airship reached 19.61 miles per hour.

Tragedy strikes in the form of death for Lt. Thomas E. Selfridge, who gained fame of sorts on September 17, 1908, as the first man killed in an aircraft accident. The pilot, Orville Wright, barely escaped with his life. The propeller shown in the case (*bottom left*) was on that 1908 Flyer. Pictures of the 1909 Wright Flyer are of the trial flights prior to the plane's being accepted and designated as Signal Corps Airplane No. 1. A diorama depicting an early flight is in the window to the right.

The museum has several dioramas such as the one depicted here. (A diorama is a three-dimensional picture with small figures placed so they blend with the painted background.) The skeleton tower is part of the system to catapult the Flyer down a track and into the air. The aircraft was moved on the ground by means of the wheels shown near the tower. This scene depicts the Wright 1909 Flyer at Fort Myer, Va.

This diorama explains the theory of flight. Push the button and the plane rises. As it goes through various maneuvers, the description above it lights up in explanation.

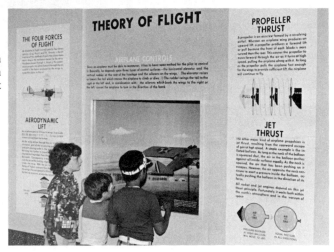

Lt. Benjamin D. Foulois transported the 1909 Flyer to Fort Sam Houston and taught himself to fly it even though he had never made a solo flight, takeoff, or landing. On March 2, 1910, he made his first flight and by September had flown the plane on sixty-one "hops." In 1911 the plane was retired from service.

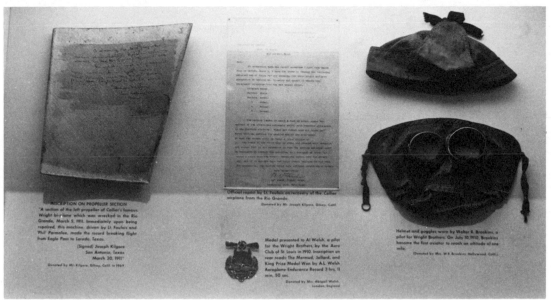

Following the retirement of the 1909 Flyer, Mr. M. R. Collier, owner of *Collier's Magazine,* loaned the Army a new 1910 Wright "B" airplane. Pictured are a section of a propeller (*left*) from Collier's plane, which was flown by Lt. Foulois, and helmet and goggles worn by Walter R. Brookins, a pilot for the Wright brothers. In 1910 Brookins became the first aviator to reach an altitude of one mile.

Two youngsters get a closeup view of a model airplane. Displays around them feature the first weapons fired from aircraft and pilots training at early flying schools.

The first shot fired from an airplane occurred on August 20, 1910, at Sheepshead Bay racetrack near New York City. With Glenn Curtiss piloting, Lt. Jacob E. Fickel fired a rifle at a small target from an altitude of 100 feet.

Lt. Myron Crissy and Mr. Phillip O. Parmalee demonstrating the first drop of a live bomb, January 15, 1911, near San Francisco. The encased tennis ball object is one of several imitation bombs made for the Harvard-Boston Aero Meet in September 1910. Claude Grahame-White demonstrated the possibility of destroying ships by dropping bombs down their funnels.

Capt. Charles de F. Chandler (*left*) and Lt. Roy Kirtland on June 7, 1912, demonstrated the use of the Lewis machine gun in a Wright "B" Flyer.

The Army's first permanent aviation school developed from the Glenn Curtiss flying school on North Island in San Diego Bay. Three officers stationed in California were ordered to San Diego in 1911 as the first students. Later, Signal Corps Airplane No. 50, seen here, was equipped for airborne radio experiments at North Island.

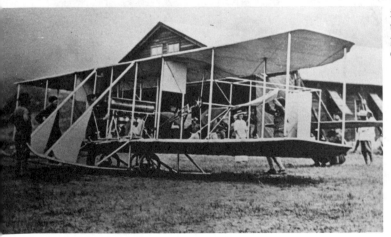

With Lt. Frank P. Lahm of the 7th Cavalry Regiment in charge, the United States opened a flying school in the Philippines on March 12, 1912, for Americans. Airplane No. 13 of the Wright "C" Series, seen here, was destroyed on its first flight with pontoons.

Further seaplane flights were conducted in the Philippines after this Burgess hydroplane, beginning takeoff run, was delivered in September 1913, but they ended in January 1915 when Lt. Herbert A. Dargue wrecked it.

Wall exhibits of memorabilia and photographs line the chronological walk through the museum. Items from the 1st Aero Squadron, created in early 1913, are seen here on the right. The enlargement from the adjoining panel shows Lt. Carl Spaatz wearing a football helmet while learning to fly in 1916 at San Diego's North Island; the airplanes here are lined up for Saturday inspection.

Revolutionary Leader Pancho Villa crossed the border from Mexico and raided Columbus, New Mexico, on March 9, 1916, killing seventeen Americans and destroying part of the town. Capt. Benjamin D. Foulois arrived there March 15 with the 1st Aero Squadron to support Brig. Gen. John J. Pershing's 15,000 ground troops. High winds, dust storms, and snowstorms thwarted the flying efforts.

Army troops survey the damage caused by Pancho Villa's raid.

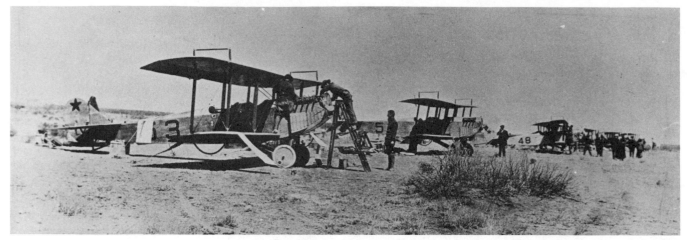

The 1st Aero Squadron used these Curtiss JN3 airplanes in Mexico. Originally the squadron there consisted of eight planes. Within a few weeks only two were operational, and these were soon condemned.

In 1916 and 1917 Curtiss produced R-3 and R-4 airplanes for the Signal Corps, some of which were used by the 1st Aero Squadron during the Pershing Punitive Expedition into Mexico. These R-3 and R-4 airplanes were powered by this type Curtiss V2-3 engine. It was replaced during World War I by the Liberty, a much more efficient engine.

The Wright 6-60 liquid-cooled engine was used by the Army in 1912/13 to power its Wright Model "C" and "D" airplanes. The 6-60 had six cylinders and was designed to produce sixty horsepower.

With its cloth skin removed, a Standard J-1 resembles a model airplane in an early stage of construction. The basic version of the J-1 was used as a trainer from 1916 to 1918.

These LWF trainers were lined up for inspection at Mineola, N.Y., in the spring of 1917. On April 5, 1917, there were fifty-six airplane pilots and fifty-one flying students in the Aviation Section. It had fewer than 250 planes, all trainers and not one suitable for carrying machine guns or bombs on a combat mission. Although war with Germany was but one day away, the Aviation Section was at least two years behind Germany in practically all aspects of military aviation. An enormous job lay ahead. The flying school in San Diego had recently been supplemented by additional schools at Mineola, N.Y.; Chicago; Memphis; and Essington, Pa. The Memphis flying school was located inside a race track. Large tents served as hangars.

★ 3 *World War I*

World War I brought a great deal of destruction to Europe from July 1914 to November 1918. Because of its isolationist policy, the United States was not directly involved until June 1917, when the first of the American Expeditionary Force landed in France. Though the Air Force Museum World War I section deals with some of the destruction, it emphasizes the men and planes of the aerial war. Artifacts, equipment, personal diaries, and photographs of legendary pilots are displayed on wall panels. Authenticity is a must, and it has been attested to by veterans of that war who have visited the museum. Of course, the eye-catching airplanes of that era are also featured. When compared later in the museum with the sleek jet aircraft, the fragile planes of World War I do seem to be mere toys.

The United States declared war on Germany in April 1917. At that time the Signal Corps's Aviation Section had 131 officers, practically all pilots and student pilots, 1087 enlisted men, and less than 250 airplanes. And none of these planes was worthy of joining the air battle. Even with the appropriation of $640 million for aeronautics by a then enthusiastic Congress, American industry was unable to produce one American-designed airplane that saw combat. With only a few airplane plants and hardly more than a dozen aeronautical engineers, the nation's resources in April 1917 were not a broad enough base on which to build and equip an effective air arm rapidly. Using a British design, United States industry did produce 3,431 DeHavilland D.H. 4s prior to the Armistice. Most were built by the Dayton-Wright Company, and 417 got into combat.

The first aerial force sent to France began arriving in Europe in September 1917. The first planes used by the First Aero Squadron on combat flights were

AR-1s. It was April 1918 before they shot down their first sky opponent. Much of the intervening time had to be spent in training. During the final seven months of the war, the gallant men who were to inspire generations to come shot down 756 enemy airplanes and 76 balloons, while losing 289 airplanes and 48 balloons to enemy fire. And they did much of the job with second-rate equipment.

Out of the combat came a new warrior—the ace—victor of five or more air battles. The United States had thirty-one, topped by Capt. Eddie Rickenbacker, the American Ace of Aces and recipient of the Medal of Honor. Career highlights of many of these heroes are depicted as the museum visitors continues their chronological walk through aviation history in the Early Years Gallery.

For nearly two years before the United States entered World War I, a number of American pilots voluntarily fought the Germans as part of the French Aviation Section. Originally known as the *Escadrille Americaine,* they changed their designation to the Lafayette Escadrille when the Germans complained. By February 1918, they had downed fifty-seven enemy aircraft while suffering nine of their own pilots killed. Raoul Lufbery and Bill Thaw perhaps were the best known of the Lafayette Escadrille.

The *Croix de Guerre* and the Legion of Honor awarded to H. S. Jones by France are displayed here. Jones is pictured with the Escadrille Lafayette standing third from the right in the accompanying photograph taken in July 1917. The legendary Lufbery is seated fourth from the right holding Whiskey (a lion), one of their mascots.

To Air Force Museum and Best Wishes to all

These French decorations were won by Eugene Bullard, the first black American to serve as a military pilot. He flew with the French Aviation Section and remained in France until World War II.

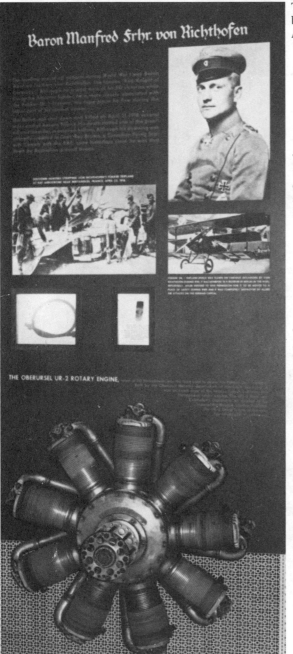

Baron Manfred Frhr. von Richthofen

THE OBERURSEL UR-2 ROTARY ENGINE.

The famous "Red Knight of Germany," more commonly known as the "Red Baron" (Manfred von Richthofen), scored most of his eighty victories while flying the Albatros fighter. He is more closely associated with the Fokker Dr. 1 triplane, which he flew during the latter part of his career.

The Fokker Dr. 1 triplane, which the Red Baron flew on various occasions during World War I, was exhibited in a museum in Berlin in the 1930s. Reportedly, Hitler refused to give permission for it to be moved to a place of safety during World War II, and it was completely destroyed by Allied air attacks on the German capital.

A variety of airplanes were used in combat long before the United States entered the war in 1917. This is a Voisin Type 5 airplane with Hotchkiss gun as photographed in 1915.

Rumpler C-IV reconnaissance airplane with flexible Parabellum gun in 1917.

British two-seater pusher airplane with swivel machine gun in front for use by the observer. This plane was shot down and captured; the victorious German pilot stands in the rear cockpit.

When the United States entered World War I, it had no military air arm capable of fighting an enemy. Although Congress appropriated $640 million for aeronautics, the United States eventually had to purchase most of its combat airplanes. Despite early failures, United States aircraft production became an outstanding success with the nation producing 50 percent more airplanes in the nineteen months it was in the war than Great Britain had produced during its thirty-one months of war.

America's greatest technological contribution was the development and mass production of the twelve-cylinder Liberty engine. It was the mainstay of the Air Service for ten years after the war. Seen here is Maj. H. H. Arnold with the first Liberty 12 engine.

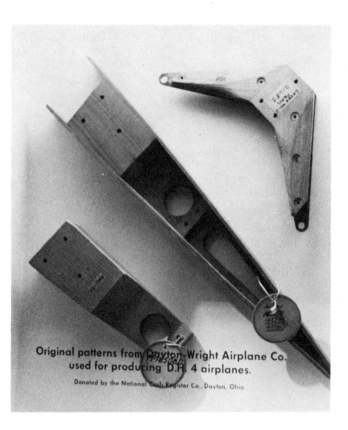

Original patterns from Dayton-Wright Airplane Co. used for producing D.H. 4 airplanes.

Donated by the National Cash Register Co., Dayton, Ohio

King George V welcomed United States troops to the British Isles with a handwritten letter that accompanies this scene in a display panel. The 211th Aero Squadron is shown arriving there on August 1,1918.

Top commanders of the Air Service were (*left to right*) Brig. Gen. Mason M. Patrick, Brig. Gen. Benjamin D. Foulois, Brig. Gen. William "Billy" Mitchell, Col. Thomas De Witt Milling, and Col. Frank P. Lahm. Major Ralph Royce, not seen here, commanded the first U.S. air unit sent to Europe, the 1st Aero Squadron, which arrived in France on September 3, 1917. Like other squadrons which gradually followed, it had to be equipped and trained.

Major Fiorello H. La Guardia, standing between two Italian officers, commanded United States Air Service personnel in Italy. He later gained fame as mayor of New York City from 1933 to 1945. The sixty-five Americans who flew with Italian aircrews in Italian airplanes represented about 25 percent of the Italian combat pilot force. The Italian primary flying course at Foggia graduated 406 U.S. cadets, most of whom were immediately transferred to France.

Perhaps the most famous U.S. World War I airplane was the Curtiss JN4-D Jenny, seen here at the museum and in flight. With America's entry into World War I on April 6, 1917, the Signal Corps began ordering large quantities of JN4s. It was generally used for primary flight training, but sometimes was equipped with machine guns and bomb racks for advanced training. After the war hundreds were sold to civilians and used during the 1920s by "barnstormers."

U.S. Air Force photo.

The DeHavilland D.H. 4 was borrowed from the British and redesigned in the United States in 1917 for the American-made Liberty engine. It was the only airplane made in the United States to get into combat, flying observation and bombing missions in 1918. Most were built by the Dayton-Wright Airplane Company.

The Spad VII, a French-designed fighter airplane, made its initial flight in July 1916. It showed such promise that it was put into production at once and used by both French and British combat squadrons. The Lafayette Escadrille was equipped with these in February 1918 when it joined the United States Air Service. This plane was restored and flown in 1962–66 at Selfridge Air Force Base, Michigan.

Captain Eddie Rickenbacker, the U.S. Ace of Aces, and a few other American pilots became well known to the American public during what has been termed the "golden age" of individual aerial combat. This famous pose was made of Rickenbacker and his Spad XIII at an aerodrome near Rembercourt, France, in September 1918. *U.S. Air Force photo.*

Captain Rickenbacker was credited with downing twenty-two enemy planes and four balloons, but probably shot down more. He was later presented the Medal of Honor by President Hoover. *U.S. Air Force photo.*

The famous Hat-in-the-Ring insignia from Captain Rickenbacker's Spad 13 is displayed at the museum along with others cut from aircraft by World War I crews. Souvenir snapshots surround the insignia. Rickenbacker's autograph appears in the base of the figure one.

When the new Air Force Museum was dedicated in 1971, Captain Rickenbacker was among the honored guests. He posed with his portrait for the *Fairborn Daily Herald.*

Dubbed "Tommy" by the pilots who flew it, the Thomas-Morse S4C Scout was the favorite single-seat training plane produced in the United States during World War I. It was used by almost every pursuit flying school in the country during 1918. Some were still being used in the mid-1930s for World War I movies filmed in Hollywood. Today, several are still being flown by aviation buffs.

Brig. Gen. William "Billy" Mitchell few this SPAD XVI as his observation and command vehicle during the latter days of the war. At the time, the SPAD XVI was one of the fastest and most maneuverable two-seaters in combat. This aircraft is on loan from the National Air and Space Museum. *U.S. Air Force photo.*

One of the world's earliest strategic bombers, the Caproni Ca. 36 was painstakingly restored in 1988-90 at the Air Force Museum. During World War I it could carry an internal bomb load of 1,800 pounds at 70 to 80 miles an hour. Some Americans who learned to fly then in Italy flew this type of aircraft, thus gaining America's early experience in strategic bombardment. *U.S. Air Force photo.*

World War I aerial combat and machine guns used in aerial duels are featured in this display. The three-dimensional scenes across the top (*left to right*) are in close-up: D.H. 4s under attack by German Fokker D. VIIs, German observation balloon being attacked by an S.E. 5, and a Spad 13 victorious over a German L.V.G. observation plane. Suspended to the left of the main display is a scaled model of the Salmson 2A.2, an extinct observation plane. The model was commissioned in 1968 by the late Eugene W. Kettering and built over an eighteen-month period by Joseph Fallo of Dayton. It features control surfaces that can be worked from the cockpit.

This actual Salmson 2A.2 was the model for the one on display. The United States procured 705 of these from the French for use by ten Air Service observation squadrons. *U.S. Air Force photo.*

During World War I Germany relied primarily on two types of machine guns to arm its airplanes. One was the Parabellum 7.92 mm (*right*) that young Anthony Fokker used in 1915 to develop the first successful system for "synchronizing" a machine gun to fire through a revolving propeller. In the 1916–1918 period, the Spandau 7.92 mm (*left*) was used almost exclusively as a fixed fuselage gun for firing through the propeller while the Parabellum was used primarily by observers as a "flexible" gun on a swivel mount.

Hatched in the trenches in France during 1918, "Stumpy John Silver" was a veteran message carrier by the time he was a few months old. When he was eleven months old, he flew into a furious German bombardment. Miraculously, he arrived twenty-five minutes later, having averaged a mile a minute, at his destination. His body was torn, but the message tube hung intact by the ligaments of his missing right leg. He was returned to health but not to battle. He was assigned to the 11th Signal Company and lived to be nearly eighteen years old at Schofield Barracks in Honolulu. His name is called on each Organization Day of the 11th Signal Company, and the senior noncommissioned officer answers, "Died of wounds received in battle in the service of his country." He stands as a symbol of the heroic and faithful service of pigeons to our combat forces during World War I.

The perfectly detailed model of the Salmson 2A.2 *(above)* seems to dominate this area of the World War I exhibit area. Full-scale aircraft in the background are the Thomas-Morse S4C Scout *(above)* and the Spad VII. The wall displays with their photographs, memorabilia, and crisp captions attract young and old alike.

Medal of Honor winners and uniforms of World War I are featured in freestanding glass cases for convenient viewing.

Regulations required Air Service officers to wear "choke" collars. But using the excuse that the prescribed collars made their necks sore from constantly turning their heads while flying, American pilots wore the British-style open-collar blouse and trousers.

Few Sopwith Camels remain today from World War I. When this F.1 exact replica was "rolled out" in December 1974 at the Air Force Museum, the second-ranking American ace to survive the war was present. Ace George Vaughn flew Camels with the 17th Aero Squadron and was credited with thirteen combat victories. He listened to the restored engine and smelled the castor oil fumes. "It's the real thing," he said.

Museum employees built their British Camel using original factory blueprints marked "confidential" and "secret." A number of the parts are from World War I. These include the 130-horsepower French Clerget rotary engine, two Vickers machine guns, George Vaughn's gunsight, and the tires and wheels.

On the fourth pull of the propeller, the Sopwith Camel's engine fired into operation. Walter J. Olsen, who headed the construction project, had the honor of sitting in the cockpit. As a safety precaution, the aircraft tail was tied down.

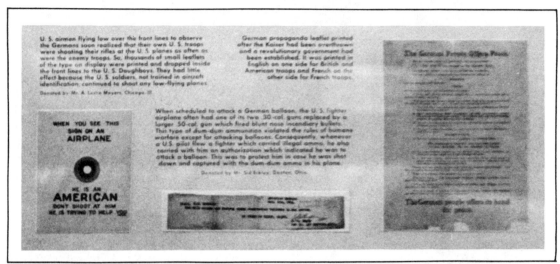

Identification posters of German airplanes hung in ready rooms for U.S. pilots to study so they could distinguish enemy from friendly aircraft. But there was another problem. American troops on the ground fired at all low-flying planes. To remedy that problem, U.S. airmen had leaflets *(left)* printed for the doughboys. They read: "When you see this sign on an airplane, he is an American. Don't shoot at him. He is trying to help YOU." The leaflets had little effect because the ground troops were not trained in aircraft identification. A German propaganda leaflet is to the right.

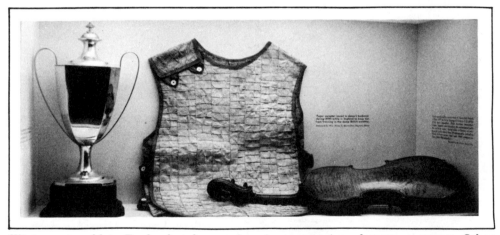

Winters are cold in England and some Americans were issued paper sweaters. Other mementos brought home include the loving cup which had been presented to the commander of the 21st Aero Squadron and a French violin which had been autographed by Capt. Eddie Rickenbacker. The violin provided entertainment at U.S. flying fields.

The World War I hall. On the right, famous names in the displays include Capt. Eddie Rickenbacker, Lt. Frank Luke, Jr., Maj. Raoul G. Lufbery, Lt. Quentin Roosevelt, and Maj. Fiorello H. LaGuardia. Roosevelt was the youngest son of former President Theodore Roosevelt and died when his Nieuport 28 was shot down behind German lines on July 14, 1918. The Germans placed a crude cross (*top right*) over his grave. On July 12, 1944, Quentin's brother, Brig. Gen. Theodore Roosevelt, Jr., died of a heart attack in Normandy following the World War II invasion of France. The two brothers are now buried side by side at Omaha Beach in France.

Museum visitors sometimes see themselves pictured in a display and are invited by the staff to autograph the photographs. Such was the case when Stephen W. Thompson of Dayton visited the museum on October 15, 1973. That's his uniform and picture in the top left. While visiting a French bombing squadron on February 5, 1918, he became the first American to shoot down an enemy airplane in World War I. Capt. William C. Lambert, America's No. 2 Ace of the war, is featured in the bottom half. While flying with the Royal Air Force in World War I he was credited with 21½ "kills," 4½ less than Capt. Eddie Rickenbacker. Lambert served with the USAF in World War II.

This is the actual insignia from the first United States Air Service observation plane to fly across enemy lines. The flight was made April 6, 1918, by Maj. Ralph Royce, commander of the 1st Aero Squadron.

Heavy clothing, boots, goggles, and a padded helmet were worn by pilots to keep warm in the air. The display card in the lower left contains pieces of fabric from Lt. Quentin Roosevelt's airplane. Next to it is an original German postcard printed and sold showing the body of Lieutenant Roosevelt beside his crashed Nieuport.

Lieutenant David E. Putnam (*photograph*) was the leading ace of the Air Service when he was shot down and killed on September 13, 1918. He had downed twelve aircraft. A control stick from a downed Fokker is displayed over a mask which was worn by Allied flyers to protect them from cold air blasts at high altitudes. First aid kits are shown bottom right.

Members of the U.S. Balloon Section made 1,642 ascensions and were aloft for 3,111 hours observing enemy activities. Although thirty-five balloons were shot down by German planes and another twelve destroyed by enemy ground fire, only one American observer was killed in 116 parachute jumps that were made. He died when pieces of his burning balloon fell on his descending parachute. The rectangular item on the left wall is a part of that balloon. Across the top is an observer's logbook for April 14 through November 15, 1918.

A long-range aerial camera being prepared for an ascent.

This is what the French landscape looked like behind the front lines.

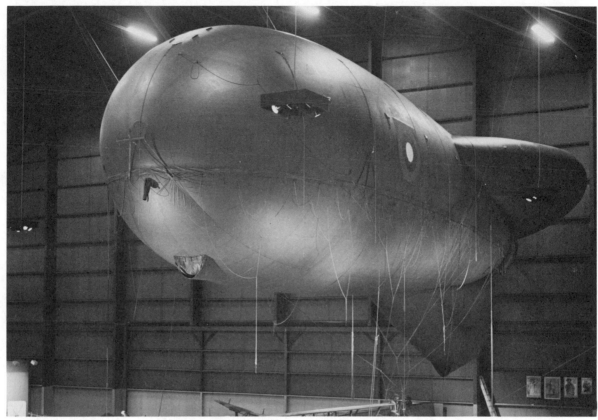

Caquot Type R balloons such as this one were used during World War I as observation platforms by the Allies. It is ninety-two feet long and thirty-two feet wide. Members of the National Association of American Balloon Corps Veterans discovered it in possession of the Royal Aircraft Establishment in England, which donated it to the museum in 1976. The Goodyear Aerospace Corporation, which had manufactured such balloons in World War I, assisted museum personnel in the restoration. *U.S. Air Force photo.*

The world's first "guided missile," the Kettering Aerial Torpedo, was invented by Charles F. Kettering and built in Dayton in 1918 for the Signal Corps. The Kettering "Bug" took off from a dolly running along a track and was guided toward its target by a system of internal preset controls. At the predetermined time the engine shut off, the wings were released, and the "Bug" plunged to earth where its 180 pounds of explosives detonated upon impact. Less than fifty "Bugs" were completed at the time of the Armistice. The "Bug" on exhibit is a full-size reproduction built by museum personnel. Its wings stretch nearly fifteen feet.

69

One hundred and twenty-three flyers of the Air Service were captured and placed in German prisoner-of-war camps. Other American POWs included two balloonists, nineteen Americans flying with the British, ten with the French, one with the Italians, and one enlisted man who drove too close to the front. The POW camp at Villingen is at top left. Russian POWs decorated the movie theatre there (center). A funeral procession and burial of an American POW are shown across the bottom.

At the end of World War I an independent Poland was created from territory previously held by Germany, Austria, and Russia. Poland thus regained the autonomy she had lost in 1831. Almost immediately the new Polish republic was invaded by the Bolsheviks. Two World War I combat pilots, Merian C. Cooper and Cedric E. Fauntleroy, received permission to recruit former U.S. flyers for a Polish Squadron similar to the Lafayette Escadrille. Seventeen Americans volunteered and served in the Kosciuszko Squadron, named in honor of Tadeusz Kosciuszko, the Pole who had fought in the American Revolution under George Washington. The Bolshevik invasion ended in May 1921 with victory for the Poles. The occupation of Germany is shown below.

Era Between WWI and WWII

Out of World War I came hard-earned experience, new tactics and equipment, and a place for the airplane in the military structure. But the years between the World Wars became frustrating ones for the enthusiasts of military aviation. The more thoughtful air leaders had come out of the war with the belief that airpower would be the dominant weapon of the future. They had to prove their theories while handicapped by a shortage of funds. Thus they turned to staged events and spectacular feats to prove their theories.

Brig. Gen. "Billy" Mitchell demonstrated the vulnerability of seapower to air attack when in 1921 his airplanes sank three captured German ships and an obsolete and stripped American battleship. In another demonstration in 1923 his Air Service bombers sank two more obsolete U.S. battleships. To some, the lesson wasn't fully understood until the Japanese devastated the United States Navy at Pearl Harbor. Other demonstrations included coast-to-coast flights, speed dashes in flimsy pursuit aircraft, altitude records in open-cockpit biplanes, aerial refueling, and flight endurance records. Because of America's vast distances, endurance and long-range flights were emphasized.

The first in-flight refueling occurred in 1923. The next year a Curtiss pursuit plane flew across the country in twenty-two hours. Also in 1924 two Douglas World Cruisers completed the first aerial circumnavigation of the earth. Flying at a top speed of 100 miles per hour and covering 26,345 miles, the trip took 175 days to complete. But only fifteen days of actual flying time were logged. A wall exhibit built around the accomplishments of those World Cruisers dominates that portion of the Air Force Museum dealing with the period between the World Wars. In a less spectacular setting, lar setting, immediately after World War I, military pilots flew airmail routes with rebuilt D.H. 4s from the war. Many civilian pilots purchased surplus Jennies and they soon became the mainstay of colorful barnstorming tours and aerial circuses.

It was not until the 1930s that the legacy of World War I equipment was lifted from the Air Corps. Steady improvements in aircraft design and performance revived the hopes of airpower advocates. Congress in 1926 had recognized the concept of military aviation as an "offensive striking force" rather than a mere auxiliary service. The development of bombers was so accelerated, however, that pursuit aviation fell far behind. Limited funds did not permit the development of both fighters and bombers. It took the uneasy rumblings of another war in Europe to get the skeptics to look to the sky.

Visitors to the museum can relish the experiences of the open-cockpit pilots of the 1920s and 1930s as they examine and marvel at a dozen authentic airplanes from this era in the Early Years Gallery.

Five Douglas World Cruisers were built in 1923 and 1924 with the specific purpose of circumnavigating the earth by air. They were powered by Liberty engines and built so that they could be equipped with wheels or pontoons. On April 6, 1924, t*he Seattle, Chicago, Boston,* and *New Orleans (two views seen here)* headed west from Seattle, Washington. Unfortunately, the *Seattle* crashed in Alaska and the *Boston* sank at sea north of Scotland. The remaining World Cruisers were eventually joined in Nova Scotia by another airplane, named the *Boston II,* and all three continued westward to finish the epic fight in Seattle on September 28, 1924. They had covered 26,345 miles and circled the globe in four and one-half months in 371 hours flying time. The *New Orleans* was loaned to the Air Force Museum in 1957 by the Los Angeles County Museum, which recalled it three decades later.

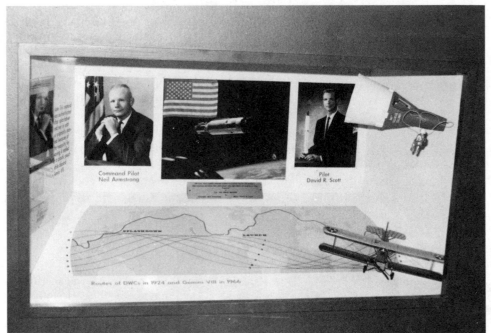

Gemini 8 astronauts carried pieces of a World Cruiser aboard their capsule when they circled the earth in 1966.

For their tremendous achievement in flying around the world, the World Cruiser flyers were awarded the coveted Mackay Trophy "for the most meritorious flight of the year." Memorialized in bronze are (*left to right*) Lieutenants John Harding, Jr., Erik Nelson, Leslie Arnold, Lowell Smith, Henry Ogden, and Leigh Wade.

The Air Service pilots succeeded after crews from Argentina, France, Great Britain, Italy, and Portugal had failed to be first to fly around the world. This trophy was presented to the United States by American Citizens of Italian Descent after the USS *Richmond* rescued four Italian flyers who were forced down in the Atlantic while attempting the feat. The *Richmond* was stationed on the route of the Douglas World Cruisers.

Pontoons were fitted on the World Cruisers near Seattle for their flight across the Pacific and along the Asian coast. They were not replaced by wheels until the planes had reached Calcutta, India.

Fifty versions of the English S.A. 5a, then known as the SE-5E, were assembled during 1922-23 in the United States by the Eberhart Steel Products Company from spare parts it had purchased. It was acquired later for the museum through a donation from the estate of Lt. Col. William C. Lambert and the Air Force Museum Foundation. Colonel Lambert, a World War I ace with 21½ victories, flew such fighters as an American member of the Royal Air Force.

The Glenn Martin bomber, built in October 1918, was too late for World War I. But it was the Air Service's first truly successful multiengine bomber design. This improved 1920 version, the MB-2, set the basic design for U.S. bombers for the decade. Using these improved bombers, Brig. Gen. Billy Mitchell arranged demonstrations in 1921 and 1923 in which obsolete German and American ships were sunk. *U.S. Air Force photo.*

In the years after World War I, more than eleven hundred obsolete D.H. 4Bs saw wide use with the Air Service, including carrying airmail for the Post Office Department. In June 1923 the Air Service successfully demonstrated in-flight refueling and two months later set a world endurance record by having a D.H. 4 stay aloft over San Diego for thirty-seven hours and fifteen minutes. *U.S. Air Force photo.*

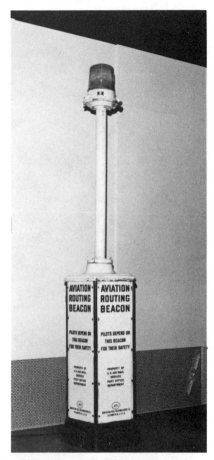

This aviation routing beacon was the property of the U.S. Air Mail Service of the Post Office Department. Its purpose was succinctly stated on its base: "Pilots depend on this beacon for their safety."

The Verville-Sperry M-1 Messenger was designed in 1919/20 at McCook Field, Dayton. It was intended to serve as an aerial dispatch carrier and to maintain liaison between field units. The hook mounted above the upper wing was used in the first successful mating of an airplane and an airship while in flight, on September 18, 1923, over Langley Field, Virginia. Lt. Rex K. Stoner flew his Messenger under a D-3 airship and "landed" on a waiting trapeze.

This Douglas 0-38F observation plane was one of the first military aircraft assigned to Alaska, landing at Ladd Field near Fairbanks in October 1940. The following June, because of engine failure, it crash landed in the wilderness. Although the pilot, Lt. Milton H. Ashkins, and the mechanic, Sgt. R. A. Roberts, hiked to safety, the 0-38 remained in the woods until June 1968 when it was brought out by helicopter. Its rescue and restoration are told by the movie box at the right.

With a welded fuselage framework of steel tubing, the Consolidated PT-1 was so sturdy and dependable that it was nicknamed the "Trusty." Procured in 1925, it was the first airplane purchased in quantity (221) since World War I. The Trusty was used extensively into the early 1930s to train pilots in California and Texas. This one was obtained in 1957 from Ohio State University.

This unique observation amphibian with an inverted Liberty engine is the Loening OA-1A, seen here in two views. Used extensively in the Hawaiian and Philippine Islands, the plane combined features of both a landplane and seaplane by merging the fuselage and hull into a single structure. Capt. Ira C. Eaker and Lt. Muir S. Fairchild piloted the *San Francisco* on a 22,000-mile Pan American good will tour of twenty-five Central and South American countries from December 21, 1926, to May 2, 1927. Four other OA-1As made the tour for which all the flights received the Mackay Trophy and Distinguished Flying Cross.

More answers to aerial refueling questions were supplied in 1929 when Maj. Carl Spaatz, Capt. Ira C. Eaker, and Lt. Elwood R. Quesada flew their Fokker C-2 for an endurance record of nearly 151 hours. They flew over the Los Angeles area between January 1 and 7 in their "Question Mark," making forty-three hookups and perfecting the refueling techniques developed in 1923. In later years, Spaatz, Eaker, and Quesada were to contribute much to the development of airpower and the Air Force. *U.S. Air Force photo.*

Although never used in combat, the Curtiss P-6E Hawk is remembered as one of the most beautiful biplanes ever built, seen here at the museum and in flight. It was a first-line pursuit aircraft of the early 1930s and was the last of the fighter biplanes built in quantity for the Army Air Corps. Despite its excellent performance, only forty-six P-6Es were ordered because of the shortage of funds during the austere days of the Depression. The museum's P-6E may be the only one of its kind in existence. It was restored by Purdue University. A Beech C-45H is in the background.

One of the best-known Air Corps fighters between the World Wars, the Boeing P-12 was first flown by military pilots as the Navy XF4B-1. This P-12E, restored at the museum, was powered by a 525-horsepower radial engine. P-12s were flown by pursuit squadrons from 1929 until replaced by Boeing P-26s in 1935.

Distinguished visitors are not uncommon at the museum. Here Lt. Gen. (Retired) James H. Doolittle *(center)* relates a personal observation to aviation history. Newscaster Lowell Thomas, historian for the Douglas World Cruisers' flight, is on the right.

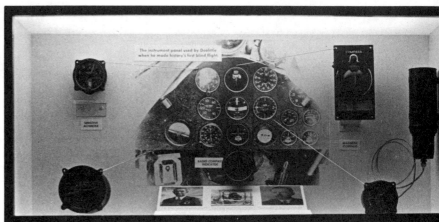

This is the instrument panel that Lt. James H. Doolittle used on September 24, 1929, when he made history's first blind flight. Years later, on April 18, 1942, Doolittle led the first U.S. bombing raid on Japan.

An improved Switlik type S-1 seat pack parachute *(left)* was used in the 1930s. It was a considerable improvement over the original parachutes designed at Dayton's McCook Field after World War I. The Army flying helmet and Navy goggles were worn aboard the Keystone biplane bomber in 1932 and 1933.

Major Thurman H. Bane piloted the first flyable helicopter on December 18, 1922. He kept it aloft for nearly two minutes at a height of six feet. A model of the multibladed machine is displayed in the case. The helicopter was designed at McCook Field by Dr. George De Bothezat and Ivan (Eremeeff) Jerome.

Medals, uniforms, and personal effects of Brig. Gen. "Billy" Mitchell, the outspoken advocate for air power, are displayed along with aerial photographs of his accomplishments. The Mark I 4,300-pound bomb *(right)* was developed for the Mitchell bombing trials on obsolete ships and tested in September 1921. However, the largest bomb he was permitted to use was a 2,000-pounder.

Mitchell's bombers sank three captured German vessels and three obsolete American battleships in 1921 and 1923 to prove that airplanes could destroy naval ships. *U.S. Air Force photo.*

This diorama depicts the LePere LUSAC-11 high altitude research airplane over McCook Field. Many aviation achievements were recorded there in the early 1920s before the Dayton facility was closed and moved approximately ten miles to the new Wright Field. In 1989 the U.S. Air Force Museum traded a P-38 to a French museum for the last remaining LUSAC-11.

Walter Beech conceived the prototype for the classic Staggerwing in 1932. By the advent of World War II, it became famous for speed, dependability, ruggedness, and flying comfort. The Staggerwing acquired its name from the negative or forward position of the lower wing. The Army Air Forces acquired 338 and designated them the UC-43 for use as utility transports.

Ten Martin B-10 bombers commanded by Lt. Col. Henry H. Arnold in 1934 flew from Washington, D.C., to Fairbanks, Alaska, and return. The B-10 was heralded as the air-power wonder of its day. It was the first all-metal monoplane bomber to be produced in quantity and could cruise at 183 miles per hour with 2,200 pounds of bombs carried internally. The aircraft on display was sold to Argentina in 1938 and donated by that country's government to the United States for the museum in 1971. This last-known remaining B-10 was painstakingly restored from 1973 to 1976 at Kelly Air Force Base, Texas, by members of the Air Force Reserve and other base volunteers. They repainted it as a B-10 used in the 1934 Alaskan Flight.

The Stearman PT-13 was typical of the biplane primary trainer used during the late 1930s and early World War II. A later version which featured a cockpit canopy was designated the PT-27. Following World War II, the Kaydet was phased out in favor of more modern trainers. The PT-13D on display was donated by the Boeing Airplane Company (which purchased the Stearman Company in 1938). It was the last Kaydet produced.

The only known surviving Seversky P-35 was restored by the Minnesota Air National Guard and presented to the Air Force Museum in mid-1974. This forerunner of the Republic P-47 was the first single-seat, all-metal pursuit plane with a retractable landing gear and enclosed cockpit to go into regular service with the Air Corps. Seventy-six were received in 1937/38 and sixty more designated as P-35As, in 1940. Twenty two-seat versions were sold to the Japanese navy in 1938. These became the only American-built planes used operationally by the Japanese in World War II. The M-1 Messenger hangs from its trapeze in the background. *U.S. Air Force photo.*

★5 *World War II*

Airpower was a proved factor, proved by Hitler's Luftwaffe dive bombers, long before the United States was pushed into World War II. If there were any doubts, the Japanese erased them on December 7, 1941, with their sneak air attack on Pearl Harbor. But military airmen and leaders of the aviation industry had planned for the eventuality of war, and America met the challenge. Many of the aircraft which made victory possible for the Allies are on display at the Air Force Museum, as well as a number of German and Japanese aircraft. The gallant men who flew and maintained American and British aircraft are also remembered.

Personal items from the B-25 crews who raided Japan on April 18, 1942, are at the museum. It was these Doolittle Raiders who flew off an aircraft carrier to give the Japanese an idea of the consequences they were to reap for Pearl Harbor. And Air Force bombers, fighters, and transports flew to Europe. They gradually and determinedly stormed and pounded their way across the continent until the skies belonged to the Allies. Airpower could then concentrate its strength in the Pacific.

China and Burma were starting to benefit from the airlift that extended over the hazardous Himalayas, or the "Hump" route as it was known. United States forces had been island-hopping, but once again they were attacking the Japanese homeland, destroying industrial and military targets which supported the far-flung Japanese forces. General H. H. Arnold's 20th Air Force, in particular, hammered aircraft production and oil supply centers. With Japan reeling from these attacks, Air Force B-29s delivered knockout blows—atomic bombs—on August 6 and 9, 1945. Japan on August 10 decided to surrender. With an invasion of the

Japanese homeland no longer necessary, a million American lives and a million Japanese lives had been spared.

The second and final atomic bomb dropped on Japan fell from a Boeing B-29 Superfortress named the *Bockscar.* It is on display at the Air Force Museum, along with actual casings of Little Boy and Fat Man, the two bombs that ended World War II.

Long before the war ended, President Franklin D. Roosevelt had directed that the U.S. Strategic Bombing Survey be established to study the results of United States bombing in Europe. Briefly stated, the Survey concluded: "Allied airpower was decisive in the war in western Europe. Hindsight inevitably suggests that it might have been employed differently or better in some respects. Nevertheless, it was decisive. In the air, its victory was complete; at sea, its contribution, combined with naval power, brought an end to the enemy's greatest naval threat—the U-boat; on land it helped turn the tide overwhelmingly in favor of Allied ground troops. . . ."

In mid-August 1945, President Truman requested a similar study of the air war against Japan. The Pacific Survey concluded: "The experience of the Pacific war supports the findings of the Survey in Europe that heavy, sustained and accurate attack against carefully selected targets is required to produce decisive results when attacking an enemy's sustaining resources. It further supports the findings in Germany that no nation can long survive the free exploitation of air weapons over its homeland. For the future it is important fully to grasp the fact that enemy planes enjoying control of the sky over one's head can be as disastrous to one's country as its occupation by physical invasion." Findings of the surveys have been reemphasized many times since then.

The visitor now makes his sojourn through those portions of the museum displaying planes, photographs, and personal memorabilia from the war. These areas include the last corridor of the Early Years Gallery and much of the Air Power Gallery.

From the company that produced Charles A. Lindbergh's *Spirit of St. Louis* came one of the sturdiest and most popular trainers of World War II: the Ryan PT-22 Recruit. Prior to 1939 the Air Corps relied completely on biplanes as primary trainers, but it found the Twenty-Two fully satisfied its requirements. This PT-22 was donated to the museum in the memory of Chief Warrant Officer Nicholas A. Romano, Jr., who lost his life while flying with the Army in Vietnam in 1968. He had served as an enlisted man in the Air Force for twenty-two years prior to retiring from the USAF and enlisting in the Army to become a pilot.

The Japanese attack on Pearl Harbor on December 7, 1941, pushed the United States into World War II. This section of the museum features the nation's recruiting and training efforts on behalf of its military forces.

One of the first heroes of the war was Capt. Colin P. Kelly, Jr. This oil painting includes his B-17 bomber.

Newspaper headlines carried a series of defeats for the United States and its Allies as Japanese forces swept through the Southwest Pacific in the early months of 1942. When they attacked the Philippines, it was defended by only seventy-two American P-40Es, fifty-two obsolete P-35As, and twelve obsolete P-26s. The P-35s had been built for export to Sweden and some still carried Swedish markings when pressed into service.

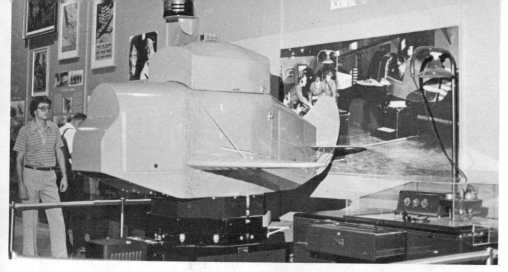

Pilots received a portion of their aerial training in the earthbound Link trainer. Here they could safely practice instrument-flying techniques.

The air war against the Japanese and the Nazis is graphically presented in the main World War II display area. Historical photographs and maps, memorabilia donated by survivors and relatives, and crisp captions relate the story of the American struggle to restore freedom. A wing of the gigantic B-36 looms overhead.

American campaigns in Europe and Africa are portrayed along the right wall. The exploits of Ohioan Don Gentile are recognized in the vertical glass case. He was one of the Army Air Force's leading aces with 27.8 enemy planes destroyed. Gen. Dwight D. Eisenhower called him a "one man Air Force."

Flaps extended to assist in its takeoff, the first B-25 starts to lift from the aircraft carrier Hornet with Jimmy Doolittle at the controls. This raid in 1942 warned the Japanese that their homeland was not free from attack.

More than 1,000 women—1,074 to be exact—earned their wings as WASPs—Women's Air Force Service Pilots—between 1942 and late 1944 under the direction of Jacqueline Cochran. They freed men for combat as they performed a variety of missions. They logged sixty million miles, flight testing new aircraft, ferrying fighters and bombers to embarkation fields, towing targets for combat pilots and ground batteries to shoot at, and training other pilots in instrument navigation. Thirty-eight were killed serving their nation. Some of their contributions, as well as uniforms, are displayed.

These WASP pilots took B-17 transition training at Lockbourne, Ohio. "Pistol Packin' Mama" is painted on the nose of the Flying Fortress. *U.S. Air Force photo.*

As they did prior to World War I, American volunteers flew with their Allies prior to the Second World War. These panels and cases illustrate their contributions to the Chinese through the Flying Tigers and to the British through the Eagle Squadrons. Nazi war art also is included.

This device controlled the altitude of fire balloons, which the Japanese launched to drift across the Pacific Ocean to harass the United States. Fuses and black powder charges circled the frame.

Developed in 1938 by Fairchild, the PT-19A Cornell was to satisfy a military requirement for a rugged monoplane primary trainer. It was ordered into quantity production in 1940. Some were powered by the Continental radial engine and designated PT-23, others with cockpit canopies were PT-26s. Of the 7,742 Cornells manufactured for the Army Air Forces, 4,889 were PT-19s. Additional Cornells were supplied to Canada, Norway, Brazil, Ecuador, and Chile.

The Vultee BT-13 Valiant was the standard basic trainer used by the Army Air Forces during World War II. Compared to the primary trainers in use at that time, it was considerably more complex. It not only had a more powerful engine, but it was faster and heavier. In addition, it required the student pilot to use two-way radio communication with the ground and to operate landing flaps and a two-position variable pitch propeller. A BT-13B is displayed.

Two distinctly different roles in Air Force history fell to the North American T-6 Texan, seen here in two views. It was one of the most widely and best-known trainers used in World War II. In the Korean conflict, the Texan became a combat plane, marking enemy positions, and was dubbed the Mosquito. Despite (or perhaps, because of) its slow speed in a jet-age war, few were lost to enemy action. The T-6G on display was received from the Pennsylvania Air National Guard. *U.S. Air Force photo.*

The Spitfire was one of the most famous airplanes of World War II, with 20,351 built from 1938 to 1948. Another 2,408 were built as Seafires for operation from aircraft carriers. This Spitfire was donated to the U.S. Air Force in 1958 by the Royal Air Force.

After World War II, Spain built the HA-1112-MIL until 1958. Except for its Rolls-Royce engine, it was almost identical to the German-built Messerschmitt Bf 109, which was first flown in 1935. This model was donated to the museum by the Spanish Air Force in 1966 and restored during 1982–1983 to the Bf 109G configuration. *U.S. Air Force photo.*

Germany first built its Junkers JU-52, seen here centered and alone, in the 1930s, yet it remained in service for more than a quarter of a century. It was obsolete as a bomber by 1939, but continued to serve throughout World War II as a versatile workhorse of the Nazi transport fleet. For a period, Adolf Hitler used a JU-52 as his private transport. Almost 500 JU-52s participated in the historic airborne assault on the island of Crete in May of 1941, and Junkers later supplied Rommel's armored forces in North Africa. Approximately thirty different countries have flown JU-52s. The one on display was donated to the museum by the Spanish government in 1971. Left is the nose of the HE-111 and right the tail of the JU-88D-1. Most aircraft exhibited outdoors were moved in 1977 to two old hangers to avoid deterioration. It is a short drive to this Annex by free shuttle bus.

Germany started developing the Heinkel HE-111 medium bomber in 1934 as a commercial airliner, but from the first the design revealed military characteristics. Eventually the bomber was also used as a paratroop transport, torpedo plane, glider tug, trainer, and aerial launcher for V-1 flying bombs. This aircraft was received in 1971 from the Spanish government, which had built many under license in World War II.

The German Junkers JU-88 Zerstörer was one of the most versatile airplanes of World War II. It was used in practically every kind of combat role, even as a "pilotless missile." It made its first flight on December 21, 1936, and hundreds were still in use in 1945. The airplane on display is a JU-88D-1, a long-range photo reconnaissance version. On July 22, 1943, the *Baksheesh* was flown to Cyprus by a defecting Rumanian Air Force pilot. It was then flown by U.S. pilots to Wright Field where it was tested extensively. It was given to the museum in 1960. *U.S. Air Force photo.*

Britain's best fighter, the Mark V Spitfire, lost its superior role when the Germans introduced the Focke-Wulf FW-190 to combat in September 1941. Two years later, powered by a longer and more powerful engine, the FW-190D took on U.S. bombers. More than twenty thousand FW-190s of all types were built. The FW-190D-9 on display was captured and brought to the United States for testing. Overhead is the U.S. duplicate of the German V-1 buzz bomb. Between June 12 and August 31, 1944, the Germans launched 8,564 against London. Usually catapulted from an inclined ramp, the V-1 was controlled in flight by internal guidance and could fly at night or during poor weather when interception was difficult.

One of the best all-around fighters in the Pacific was the Kawanishi N1K2-J Shiden-Kai George 21, produced during the last year of World War II by the Japanese. Only 428 were built because of initial production problems and later shortages of parts resulting from B-29 raids on Japan. The George 21 on display was donated by the City of San Diego in 1959 through the cooperation of the Air Force Association.

Developed from a 1938 design, the Messerschmitt Me-262 Schwalbe (Swallow) was the world's first operational turbojet aircraft. When initially flown as a pure jet on July 18, 1942, it proved to be much faster that conventional airplanes. More than 1,400 were built, but fewer than 300 saw combat. Allied bombers destroyed hundreds on the ground—much to the relief of other Allied aircrews. This Schwalbe was brought to the U.S. in 1945 for flight evaluation and was restored in 1976-79 at Kelly Air Force Base, Texas.

The Westland Lysander III is best known for its "cloak-and-dagger" role, flying agents in and out of German-occupied Europe for the Royal Air Force. The United States acquired three, probably for evaluation, and twenty-five more were assigned to the 8th Air Force for target towing. Mr. Dwight F. Brooks of West Los Angeles restored and flew this aircraft and later donated it to the Museum. Nose of the Beech UC-43 Staggerwing is to the right. *U.S. Air Force photo.*

94

The first Curtiss P-36A Hawk delivered to the Air Corps in 1938 is exhibited with the "desert sand and spinach" camouflage of the 27th Pursuit Squadron. Two of the first six Army Air Corps fighters to get off the ground to meet the enemy at Pearl Harbor on December 7, 1941, were P-36s. The outmoded P-36 was soon relegated to training and courier duties within the United States.

Initial flights of the Bell P-39 Airacobra were made at Wright Field in April 1939. Its unique engine location behind the cockpit (note the air intake) at first was a cause for concern for some pilots. Bell built 9,584 Airacobras with 4,773 being allotted to the Soviet Union. This P-39Q was obtained by the Air Force Museum Foundation from the Hardwick Aircraft Company in El Monte, California.

Two views of Lockheed's P-38 Lightning designed in 1937 as a high-altitude interceptor. In Italy and the Mediterranean, New Guinea and the South Pacific, North Africa and the Aleutians, this two-engine, twin-tailed terror of the skies wrote aviation history. The P-38 was the most versatile fighter of World War II, and American flyers affectionately dubbed it the "round-trip ticket." One Lightning returned to base on a single engine five times. The Germans during the North African campaign named it the Forked-Tail Devil. *U.S. Air Force photo.*

Culver Aircraft Corporation was the major producer of radio-controlled target aircraft, such as this PQ-14B, during World War II. They were used to train anti-aircraft artillery gunners. A pilot occupied the cockpit only on ferry or check flights. Mr. Robert E. Parcell of Fort Worth donated this aircraft. *U.S. Air Force photo.*

According to legend the Japanese were afraid of sharks. To this end, World War II pilots painted their Curtiss P-40 Warhawks as shown in these three views. The legend has not been substantiated, but the Warhawk did have an outstanding record in downing 286 Japanese planes in an eight-month period, while only eight Warhawks were lost. The plane saw action on every fighting front of the war and was flown by the famed Flying Tigers as well as the first Army Air Forces black unit, the 99th Fighter Squadron. The airplane on display is one of the few P-40Es still in existence.

U.S. Air Force photo.

The Republic P-47 Thunderbolt was one of America's leading fighter planes of World War II. An auxiliary fuel tank permitted the P-47 to escort heavy bombers far into German territory. Not only was it an impressive high-altitude escort fighter, the P-47 gained recognition as a low-level fighter-bomber because of its ability to absorb battle damage and keep flying. Republic Aviation Corporation donated the P-47D on exhibit.

U.S. Air Force photo.

Two coaxial contrarotating propellers are featured on this Fisher P-75A Eagle, which is on loan from the National Air and Space Museum. The engine has twenty-four cylinders. Only fourteen aircraft of two models were built before the program was cancelled in late 1944.

This P-47 throttle quadrant is pictured alongside the Republic Thunderbolt. The display is one of several that visitors are permitted to operate.

The only known remaining North American A-36, produced in 1942, is on display at the museum. It is described as the dive bomber version of the P-51A Mustang. The extended dive brakes (visible on the left wing) insured better stability in dives. This A-36A was restored for the museum in 1974 by the Minnesota Air National Guard at Duluth.

Margie H, whose colors were used for the A-36, was credited with twenty-five combat missions against Germany, as well as with two Nazi aircraft downed.

North American's P-51 Mustang could certainly be considered an international fighter. It was designed to British specifications by engineers formerly with Fokker and Messerschmitt. It gained fame with the U.S. Army Air Forces using a British engine. With the aid of external fuel tanks, it met Luftwaffe interceptors deep inside German territory and repeatedly scored heavily over the enemy planes. The P-51D on display was obtained from the West Virginia Air National Guard in 1957. It was the last USAF propeller-driven fighter in operation.

U.S. Air Force photo.

NORTHROP P-61C "BLACK WIDOW"

The heavily-armed Black Widow was this country's first aircraft specifically designed as a night fighter. In the nose, it carried radar equipment which enabled its crew of two or three to locate enemy aircraft in total darkness and fly into proper position to attack.

The XP-61 was flight-tested in 1942 and delivery of production aircraft began in late 1943. The P-61 flew its first operational intercept mission as a night fighter in Europe on July 3, 1944 and later was also used as a night intruder over enemy territory. In the Pacific, a Black Widow claimed its first "kill" on the night of July 6, 1944. As P-61s became available, they replaced interim Douglas P-70s in all US-AAF night fighter squadrons. During WWII, Northrop built approximately 700 P-61s; 41 of these were -Cs manufactured in the summer of 1945 offering greater speed and capable of operating at higher altitude. Northrop fabricated 36 more Black Widows in 1946 as F-15A unarmed photo-reconnaissance aircraft.

The Black Widow on display was presented to the Air Force Museum by the Tecumseh Council, Boy Scouts of America, Springfield, Ohio, in 1958. It is painted and marked as a P-61B assigned to the 550th Night Fighter Squadron serving in the Pacific in 1945.

SPECIFICATIONS

Span	66 ft.
Length	49 ft. 7 in.
Height	14 ft. 8 in.
Weight	35,855 lbs. loaded
Armament	Four .50-cal. machine guns in upper turret and four 20mm cannon in belly; 6,400 lbs. of bombs
Engines	Two Pratt & Whitney R-2800s of 2,100 hp. each

PERFORMANCE

Maximum speed	425 mph
Cruising speed	275 mph
Range	1,200 miles
Service ceiling	46,200 ft.
Cost	$170,000

99

Somewhere in France during World War II, armament men load 20mm shells into a box for the P-61 in the background. The shells were fired from four cannon in the belly of the Black Widow night fighter.

Pictured are the Bell P-63A Kingcobra and overhead the Fuji Hikoki MXY7 Ohka suicide bomb. The Kingcobra was a World War II fighter; however, most were sent to Russia and the Free French as lend-lease material. Some were utilized by the United States for fighter training. The Ohka (Cherry Blossom), a Japanese suicide weapon, was particularly effective against U.S. naval forces during the invasion of Okinawa in April 1945. The Ohka was carried to the vicinity of its target beneath a "mother" aircraft. Upon release, the Ohka pilot glided toward its target. When in position he fired the rocket engine and dived at high speed into his victim, perishing in the resulting explosion.

America's first jet-propelled airplane made its initial flight on October 1, 1942. Development of Bell's P-59 Airacomet was ordered personally by Gen. H. H. Arnold on September 4, 1941, and the project was conducted under the utmost secrecy. Bell produced sixty-six P-59s. Although the airplane's performance was not spectacular and it never got into combat, it provided training for AAF people and invaluable data for subsequent development of higher performance jet airplanes. A P-59B is exhibited.

The 1-A was America's first jet engine. Copied from the highly secret British Whittle jet engine, it had a thrust of only 1,650 pounds. The British provided the plans for the Whittle to America in 1941 and General Electric was requested to make a U.S. version. The work was conducted under such secrecy that many people employed on the project believed that they were building a turbosupercharger. At the same time Bell was requested to build an airplane that could use it. The result was America's first jet-propelled airplane: the P-59.

Similar in lines to the propeller-driven Bell P-63 Kingcobra, the jet-powered Bell P-59A Airacomet never reached the operational stage of its "old-fashioned" sister. The P-63 was widely used by the Russian Air Force in support of ground troops. *U.S. Air Force photo.*

This prisoner of war display is the most extensive of the several on view at the museum. Many of the original items in the case are from Stalag Luft I, Barth, Germany, a Luftwaffe camp for captured American fliers.

The center of attraction in this display is the colorful portrait of a "Dream Girl" painted in calcimine by Lt. Marvin Haskins on a piece of plywood from a Canadian Red Cross food box. It was hung in a Stalag Luft I mess hall in 1944/45, and her visionary face gradually became the symbol to each POW of his girl back home.

An enlarged exhibit honoring the Major Glenn Miller Army Air Force Band was dedicated on July 3, 1976. Special guests for the event were Ray McKinley *(left)*, who became leader of the famed group after Miller's untimely death in 1944, and Johnny Desmond, who was the lead vocalist for many years. "Next to letters from home, the Glenn Miller Army Air Force Band was the greatest morale builder we had in the European Theater of Operations," reported Lt. Gen. James H. Doolittle. After the dedication, the current Glenn Miller Band performed for a crowd of 10,000 persons in a setting reminiscent of a bygone era.

Hanging from the ceiling of the large bay is this Taylorcraft L-2M Grasshopper. Such light planes were used in World War II for liaison and reconnaissance. An Aeronca L-3B Grasshopper, similar in appearance to the L-2M, is also part of the museum collection.

During World War II the Curtiss O-52 Owl was used for courier missions within the United States and for short-range submarine patrol over the Gulf of Mexico as well as the Atlantic and Pacific oceans. The plane on display was received from the U.S. Federal Reformatory at Chillicothe, Ohio, in 1962. Inside, painted on a bulkhead in the cockpit was the statement, "Help, I'm being held a prisoner."

The aircraft on display is one of 432 Expeditors that Beech rebuilt as C-45Hs. The C-45 was the World War II military version of the popular Beechcraft Model 18 commercial light transport. Beech built a total of 4,526 of these aircraft for the AAF between 1939 and 1945 in four versions: the AT-7 Navigator navigation trainer, the AT-11 Kansas bombing-gunnery trainer, the C-45 Expeditor utility transport, and the F-2 for aerial photography and mapping.

Student bombardiers, working in the nose of the Beech AT-11 Kansas, normally dropped 100-pound bombs filled with sand. About 90 percent of the Air Corps's 45,000 bombardiers were trained in AT-11s during World War II. This aircraft was donated to the museum by the Abrams Aerial Survey Corporation of Lansing, Michigan. *U.S. Air Force photo.*

U.S. Air Force photo.

The Curtiss C-46 Commando gained fame during World War II transporting cargo over the "Hump," the Himalayas, from India to China after the Japanese had occupied Burma. C-46s saw additional service during the Korean conflict. The C-46D on display was retired from service in Panama in 1968, stored at Davis-Monthan AFB in Arizona, and flown to the museum in May 1972. The circular insignia is that of the Air Transport Command of the U.S. Army Air Force. *U.S. Air Force photo.*

Markings on this Waco CG-4A glider are those used during the D-Day invasion of France on June 6, 1944. Hundreds of these gliders were towed across the English Channel by C-47s, landing behind German coastal defenses. An individual Waco could carry fifteen soldiers or either a jeep, a quarter-ton truck, or a 75mm howitzer. This glider was unveiled at the museum one day ahead of the thirty-second anniversary of the Normandy invasion. The Bell P-59B is also shown.

Gen. Matthew B. Ridgway *(center)* commanded the 82nd Airborne Division during World War II and used the Waco CG-4A glider during the invasion of Sicily in 1943 and Normandy a year later. The Army general participated in the 1976 unveiling ceremony for the glider at the Air Force Museum. He is shown here in the cockpit being interviewed for television.

Student glider pilots normally received about six hours of dual instruction in the Schweizer TG-3A training glider before being trained in the large CG-4A cargo glider. The TG-3A's wing is made of spruce and mahogany plywood covered with doped fabric. Henry A. Shevchuk of Cadogan, Pennsylvania, donated this glider to the museum. It was restored by the Sparton School of Aeronautics, Tulsa, Oklahoma.

Nearly 2,900 of these Fieseler Fi 156-1 Storch (Stork) aircraft were built for the German Air Force between 1937 and 1945. One of these light aircraft rescued deposed dictator Benito Mussolini from a rock-strewn Italian plateau. The airplane on display is painted as the one used by Field Marshal Erwin Rommel in North Africa. It was donated to the museum by Lt. Col. Perry A. Schreffler and Maj. Robert C. Van Ausdell, both of the U.S. Air Force Reserve.

This is the engine that powered the "Vengeance Weapon" developed by Germany during the war and fired against London and other city populations. Approximately 6,500 were manufactured during 1944/45. They had a maximum range of 220 miles, ceiling of 55 miles, and a speed of 3,500 miles per hour. Liquid oxygen and alcohol were used as propellants.

Visitors to the museum relive the news of the invasion of Europe and the eventual downfall of Nazi Germany.

After two years of testing and development, the Sikorsky R-4 Hoverfly was first used in combat in May 1944. The world's first production helicopter had shown such promise that the AAF ordered 100 R-4Bs. The one hanging from the ceiling of the museum was donated in 1967 by the University of Illinois. It has three rotor blades.

Skytrain is its official name, but the C-47 is more popularly known as the Gooney Bird. It was adapted from the DC-3, which appeared in 1936. During World War II it was used to carry troops and cargo, and to tow gliders. During the Vietnam conflict, the Gooney Bird was outfitted with machine guns to become Puff the Magic Dragon.

Six American crews and six British crews flew twelve Douglas A-20 Havoc planes on the first U.S. daylight bombing raid in Europe. It was a low-altitude mission against four Dutch airfields used by the Germans. The versatile A-20 attack bomber was used in the Pacific, Middle East, North African, Russian, and European theatres. The A-20G on display was donated by the Bankers Life and Casualty Company of Chicago. It was the first series to have a "solid" nose.

U.S. Air Force photo.

Consolidated's B-24 Liberator was employed in every combat theatre during the war. B-24s conducted one of the most famous raids of the war on August 1, 1943, against the oil refinery complex at Ploesti, Rumania. The raid set a record which still stands for the most Medals of Honor awarded in a single battle—five. The B-24D on exhibit is the same type airplane as the *Lady Be Good,* the world-famous B-24D which disappeared on a mission from North Africa in April 1943 and which was found in the Libyan Desert in May 1959. Volunteer museum tour guides who escort school groups refer to this plane as the *Strawberry Lady.*

U.S. Air Force photo.

The North American B-25 Mitchell was one of the most famous bombers of the war. The plane was named after Brig. Gen. Billy Mitchell, a pioneer advocate of military airpower. It gained its greatest fame on April 18, 1942, when sixteen B-25Bs, launched from the carrier USS *Hornet,* raided Tokyo in the first reprisal by U.S. forces against the Japanese mainland. North American rebuilt the plane on display to the configuration of a Tokyo Raider.

U.S. Air Force photo.

U.S. Air Force photo.

The Air Corps ordered 1,131 Martin B-26 Marauders in September 1940 because the plane had such good speed, range, and ceiling. Bombing from medium altitudes of 10,000 to 15,000 feet, the Marauder had the lowest loss rate of any Allied bomber—less than one-half of one percent. In 1945 when B-26 production was halted, 5,266 had been built. The B-26G on display was flown in combat by the Free French during the final months of World War II. It was obtained from the Air France training school in 1965.

First flown in 1939, the Douglas B-23 Dragon incorporated many features of the DC-3 commercial transport and was developed as a successor to the B-18. It was soon outclassed by more modern bombers, and the thirty-eight that were built were used in support roles. Several were still flying as private cargo transports in the early 1980s. *U.S. Air Force photo.*

The Douglas A-26 Invader, including the B-26, flew combat missions in three wars, over a twenty-six-year span. It was used in World War II for level bombing, ground strafing, and rocket attacks. In 1948 it was redesignated the B-26 and used as a night intruder, harassing North Korean supply lines. During the Vietnam conflict it was used as a night interdiction aircraft along the Ho Chi Minh Trail. The A-26C on display appears in the colors and markings used during the Korean conflict.

U.S. Air Force photo.

One of the most famous airplanes ever conceived was designed by the Boeing Aircraft Company in 1934. The B-17 Flying Fortress made its maiden flight in 1935, in an era when practically all other bombers had two engines or less. Lt. Col. Robert D. Olds in February 1938 led six B-17s on a flight from Miami to Buenos Aires and set a new record for distance. One of the pilots was 1st Lt. Curtis E. LeMay, who ultimately became the Air Force chief of staff. The B-17 was used in every combat zone of World War II, particularly for daylight bombing of German industrial targets. Although only a handful of the Flying Fortresses were in service at the start of the war, nearly 13,000 had been constructed by May 1945 when production was halted. A B-17G is on display at the museum.

U.S. Air Force photo.

An airman gunner protected the B-17 from attack from the rear with twin stinger .50 caliber machine guns. The Flying Fortress had thirteen such guns for self-protection.

This Boeing B-29 Superfortress, on display at the Air Force Museum, brought World War II to an end and halted the further loss of American lives. It is this aircraft from which the second atomic bomb was dropped on Japan. When Nagasaki was devastated on August 9, 1945, the Japanese government was finally convinced it must surrender.

From Salt Lake City, where the *Bockscar* crew had trained, to Nagasaki, where they demonstrated the proficiency of their training. That was the route of this famous B-29. It was named for Capt. Frederick C. Bock, the pilot, who switched planes and flew the *Great Artiste,* an instrument plane, for the eventual raid.

Engineering knowledge gained from the early XB-15, XB-19 and the war-proved B-17 led to the development of the Superfortress. Technological breakthroughs of this aircraft, coupled with the simultaneous development of the atomic bomb, ushered in a new era in warfare and strategic airpower. But man was still required in the cockpit.

Gen. Douglas MacArthur *(large photograph)* accepted the Japanese surrender aboard the USS *Missouri* on September 20, 1945, in Tokyo Bay. The panel left of center includes a profile photograph of the B-29 from which the final atomic bomb was dropped. That aircraft now is displayed in the museum.

This is one of two Nazi bronze eagles that once stood above the entry to Adolf Hitler's office at the Reich Chancellery. The sculpting and casting are considered to be of the highest quality and were done by the Schmidt-Ehmen Foundry in Munich in 1938. Maj. Gen. Edmund W. Hill, then a colonel, "liberated" the eagle in 1945 to win a $10 bet. The other eagle was taken by the Russians and its fate is unknown.

Although the war had ended, not all Americans returned home. The B-24 *Lady Be Good* crew members perished in the African desert in 1943, but their fate was not discovered until 1959. Their courage is depicted here and in the Chapel exhibit.

This is the type of aircraft, the Noorduyn UC-64A Norseman, that bandleader Major Glenn Miller was flying as a passenger when it disappeared December 15, 1944, between England and Paris. It was a ten-place utility transport designed by a Canadian firm for use in arctic areas, but also used in the European and Pacific theaters. Manufacturing continued from the late 1930s to the early 1950s.

"Bamboo Bomber" and "Rhapsody in Glue" were just two of the nicknames for the Cessna UC-78 Bobcat, whose earlier models were known as the AT-17 and AT-8. The fuselage framework was made of welded chrome-moly steel tubing, shaped with wooden formers and fairing strips, and then covered with doped fabric. It normally could carry one pilot and four passengers.

In September 1939 the Douglas B-18 Bolo was the standard bomber for the United States, although it was greatly inferior in performance to the four-engine B-17, which cost more and whose production had been limited to only twenty-three. By the time of Pearl Harbor, the B-18 was obsolete. This one is shown being restored at the museum. A Douglas 0-46A, shown overhead, was one of ninety ordered in 1935 and is the only remaining example of its kind.

The Jet Age

After victory in World War II, the importance of the airman and his machine was proved beyond doubt. The Jet Age had arrived and it was clear that future defense would depend largely on technological superiority. In October 1942 the XP-59A jet aircraft made its first flight. Development of this revolutionary aircraft was shrouded in secrecy, to the point of placing a wooden propeller on the nose to confuse enemy espionage efforts.

With knowledge gained from the XP-59A, a version of which is on display at the Air Force Museum in the Air Power Gallery, development of the Lockheed F-80 Shooting Star began in 1942. But operational models had reached the Air Force too late for World War II. Nevertheless, the F-80 is assured a lasting place in aviation history as the first jet accepted for operational service within the Air Force. With it, the Jet Age became a reality for America. The Shooting Star on display at the museum was specially modified for racing by equipping it with a smaller canopy, a shorter wing, and redesigned air intakes.

Perhaps the world's most exotic jet airplane is the North American XB-70 Valkyrie, which dominates the experimental aircraft area of the Modern Flight Gallery. This six-engine jet bomber was conceived in the 1950s to fly at three times the speed of sound. Because of fund limitations, only two were built, both for the advance study of aerodynamics and propulsion as related to large supersonic aircraft. The Valkyrie on display is the only surviving XB-70. It flew as a research ship from September 1964 until it was flown to the museum in February 1969. Scientific data gathered over the years from the XB-70 have gone into the development of other jet aircraft, both military and civilian.

America's first jet airplane manufactured in large quantities was the Lockheed P-80 Shooting Star, which was redesignated the F-80 in 1948. It made its initial flight in January 1944, but was produced too late for World War II. During the Korean conflict it was used extensively for low-level attacks against ground targets. Its basic design was used for the T-33 and to a lesser degree for the F-94. The P-80R on display was modified for racing and set a world speed record in 1947 of 623.8 miles per hour.

On July 26, 1947, President Truman signed the legislation that established a new defense organization for the nation and brought an independent Air Force into being. This National Security Act of 1947, appropriately, was signed aboard the President's personal airplane. The Air Force began functioning as the nation's specialist in airpower on September 18 of that year when W. Stuart Symington was sworn in as its first secretary.

A year later, the new Air Force saw its first action under its new name. It wasn't combat. It was Operation Vittles, the airlift to save the people of West Berlin from Communist-imposed starvation. Since then, Air Force disaster relief teams have contributed to the welfare of people in many other parts of the world as well as the United States. And the Air Force has aided the civilian populace, at least indirectly, through numerous by-products of its research, development, and training.

When Communist aggression erupted in Korea in 1950, the Air Force was quick to respond. As the ground battle rolled back and forth, the Air Force once again proved the value of hitting the enemy behind the lines, providing close tactical support for ground forces and air supply for isolated land operations. It was also an air war as jet fighters edged their way into the skies and propeller-driven aircraft began to slip into the past. The struggle also produced thirty-eight Air Force aces and four Medal of Honor winners who are commemorated at the museum.

In the 1960s the Air Force was again called upon to provide close air support to ground forces, this time in Southeast Asia. American air action over South Vietnam continued from late 1961 to early 1973. In the North, it was exclusively an air war. Air Force fighter-bombers and bombers attacked military barracks, storage areas, infiltration routes, and lines of communication. Because of the longstanding White House policy of graduated escalation, they were forced to encounter the most sophisticated and concentrated air defense network ever faced in any war. And while the United States was never denied use of enemy airspace, the Air Force did not gain the clearcut air supremacy it enjoyed in World War II and Korea. Nevertheless, American ground troops never knew the demoralization of having their source of supplies cut off, of being constantly exposed to aerial reconnaissance, and of always being vulnerable to strafing and bombing. Finally, airpower forced an end to the long American involvement in Southeast Asia. Planes on display at the museum from this era include the actual A-1E which Major Bernie Fisher flew on the mission that earned him the first Medal of Honor awarded to an airman in the Southeast Asia conflict.

Jet-propelled aircraft were the mainstays of that conflict, but propeller-driven aircraft played their important support role, as they will continue to in the future. The success of all flying operations, however, remains with the vision, experience, courage, and dedication of the people who command, support, and fly them. This was demonstrated vividly in early 1991 against Iraqi forces during Operation Desert Storm. That campaign was summarized by the U.S. Air Force chief of staff as "the first time in history that a field army has been defeated by airpower." The aircraft, men, and women who have contributed over the years to jet-age history are honored mainly in the Air Power and Modern Flight Galleries.

The Lockheed T-33A Shooting Star on display was flown to the museum in 1962. The two-place aircraft was designed for training pilots already qualified to fly propeller-driven aircraft. It was developed from the single-seat F-80 by lengthening the fuselage three feet. The T-Bird, as many pilots call it, has served with the air forces of more than twenty countries.

President Truman signed the legislation that created an independent Air Force, aboard his Douglas C-54, popularly known as the *Sacred Cow*. The Air Force now celebrates its birthday on September 18, the date in 1947 when W. Stuart Symington became its first secretary.

When the Soviet Union attempted to starve and freeze the people of West Berlin, an American and British airlift delivered more than 2.3 million tons of food, fuel, and other supplies from June 1948 to July 1949. During that airlift, Lt. Gail S. Halvorsen started Operation Little Vittles by dropping candy in toy parachutes (*left panel, above*). U.S. Air Force photo.

President Truman in 1948 signed an Executive Order that banned all forms of segregation in the military. A copy of that two-page decree is displayed alongside photographs of two prominent Tuskegee airmen: Lt. Gen. Benjamin O. Davis and Gen. Daniel J. "Chappie" James, Jr.

The Air Force's first postwar fighter, the Republic F-84 Thunderjet, first flew on February 28, 1946. From 1947 to 1953 approximately 4,450 were built with "straight wings." They were used in the Korean conflict against enemy railroads, bridges, supply depots, and troop concentrations. The F-84E on display is nestled alongside a B-36.

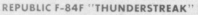

REPUBLIC F-84F "THUNDERSTREAK"

The swept-wing F-84F evolved from the straight-wing F-84. The prototype first flew on June 3, 1950 and deliveries began in 1954, primarily to the Tactical Air Command as a ground support fighter-bomber.

Republic produced 2,112 -Fs while General Motors built an additional 599. Of these, 1,301 were to NATO air forces. Production of a reconnaissance version, the RF-84F, totaled 718 aircraft, including 386 for allied countries. The RF-84F featured engine air intakes at the wing roots plus cameras in the nose.

F-84Fs gradually were replaced by supersonic F-100s in the late 1950s and were turned over to Air National Guard units. However, some F-84Fs were called back to temporary USAF service in the early 1960s due to the Berlin Crisis and the threat of Soviet missiles in Cuba.

The aircraft on display was flown to the museum in 1970 following its assignment to the Ohio ANG. During its career, it served in England, Greece, Alaska, and the continental U.S. It was one of the aircraft which participated in the mass deployment of fighters across the Atlantic in November 1961.

SPECIFICATIONS

Span . . . . 33 ft. 7 in.
Length . . . . 43 ft. 5 in.
Height . . . . 15 ft.
Weight . . . 27,000 lbs. loaded
Armament . . . . . . six .50-cal. machine guns and 24 five-inch rockets; 6,000 lbs. of bombs
Engine . . . Wright J65 of 7,220 lbs. thrust

PERFORMANCE

Maximum speed . . . . 685 mph
Cruising speed . . . . . 535 mph
Range . . . . 1,900 miles
Service ceiling . . . . 44,450 ft.

Cost $769,000

Even with the two F-84s parked by the B-36, there is ample space for additional airplanes.

LOCKHEED F-94A "STARFIRE"

The two-place F-94 was this nation's first operational jet all-weather interceptor. It was developed from the single-seat P-80 Shooting Star which had been the Army Air Forces' first operational jet aircraft procured in significant quantities. Although the F-94 had a redesigned fuselage, it used the P-80 tail, wing, and landing gear. The Starfire was also the first U.S. production jet to have an afterburner, which provided brief periods of additional engine thrust. It was equipped with radar in the nose to permit the observer in the rear seat to locate an enemy aircraft at night or in poor weather. The pilot then flew the Starfire into proper position for an attack based upon the observer's radar indications.

F-94s were primarily deployed for the defense of the United States in the early 1950,s serving with Air Defense Command squadrons. Many Air National Guard units were later equipped with F-94s.

Lockheed produced 853 F-94s for the Air Force, beginning in December 1949. Of these, 110 were F-94As. The F-94A on exhibit was transferred from active inventory to the Air Force Museum in May 1957.

SPECIFICATIONS

Span	38 ft. 9 in.
Length	40 ft. 1 in.
Height	12 ft. 2 in.
Weight	15,330 lbs.
Armament	Four .50-caliber machine guns.
Engine	General Electric J33 of 6,000 lbs. thrust with afterburner

PERFORMANCE

Max. speed	630 mph.
Cruising speed	520 mph.
Normal range	930 miles
Service ceiling	42,750 ft.

Developed by North American in 1945, the F-82 Twin Mustang was produced by "marrying" two P-51 airframes. The purpose was to provide a fighter that would have two pilots, thereby reducing fatigue on long-range escort missions to Japan. However, World War II ended before the plane went into production. With the advent of the Korean conflict, the F-82 was used as a night fighter. The first three North Korean airplanes destroyed by U.S. forces were shot down by all-weather F-82 interceptors on June 27, 1950. The F-82B on display *(front and rear view)* set a new distance record in 1947 when it was flown nonstop 5,051 miles from Hawaii to New York.

The Republic YRF-84F Thunderstreak was designed to hitch a ride on the underside of a B-36 and tag along until it was needed for photo reconnaissance. (It was also the model for the F-84F.) However, later development of mid-air refueling for range extension of fighters proved so successful that experiments with parasites were discontinued. Also shown are the F-86D, F-100A, and F-101B.

Three models of the North American F-86 Sabre are displayed at the museum, one in a unique manner—without its skin. The F-86H, with its anatomy revealed, was a fighter-bomber. The F-86A, shown with the control tower sign from Japan's Itazuke Air Base, was designed as a high-altitude day fighter. The F-86D, an all-weather interceptor, is shown in the top photograph. Its noticeable characteristic is a black nose cone containing radar and a wider air scoop beneath. During the Korean conflict, the F-86A, E, and F models shot down 829 Russian-built MIG-15s at a loss of only 58 Sabres.

NORTHROP F-89J "SCORPION"

The F-89 was a twin-engine, all-weather fighter-interceptor designed to locate, intercept, and destroy enemy aircraft by day or night under all types of weather conditions. It carried a pilot in the forward cockpit and a radar operator in the rear who guided the pilot into the proper attack position. The F-89 made its initial flight in Aug. 1948 and deliveries to the Air Force began in July 1950. Northrop produced 1,050 F-89s.

On July 19, 1957, a Genie test rocket was fired from an F-89J, the first time in history that an air-to-air rocket with a nuclear warhead was launched and detonated. 350 F-89s were converted to "J" models which became the Air Defense Command's first fighter-interceptors modified to carry nuclear armament.

The Scorpion on display was transferred to the Air Force Museum from the Maine Air National Guard and was the last F-89 in service with an operational unit.

SPECIFICATIONS

Span . . . . 60 ft. 0 in.
Length . . . . 53 ft. 10 in.
Height . . . . 17 ft. 6 in.
Weight . . . . 47,719 lbs
Armament . Two AIR-2A Genie missiles plus four AIM-4C Falcon missiles
Engines . . Two Allison J35 jet engines of 8,000 lbs. thrust each with afterburner

PERFORMANCE

Maximum speed . 630 mph.
Cruising speed . . . 465 mph.
Range . Approx. 1,000 miles
Service ceiling . . . 45,000 ft.

Inert Genie atomic rockets are carried under each wing of the F-89J on display. Framed within the tail fins of this rocket is the Wright Field laboratory which once housed an Air Force nuclear reactor.

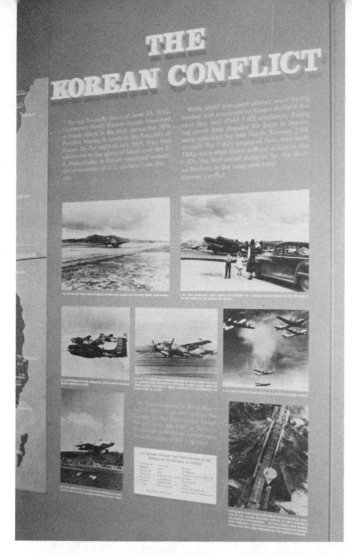

"During the early hours of June 25, 1950, Communist North Korean troops launched a sneak attack in the dark across the 38th parallel, hoping to conquer the Republic of Korea." Two days later, while four USAF F-82s were flying protective cover for American evacuees near Seoul, two North Korean YAK aircraft attacked the USAF fighters. Both of the enemy planes were shot down without an American loss. Thus began "the long and bitter Korean Conflict."

Many of the museum's exhibits, such as this one, were made possible by donations from individuals who contributed in some measure to aviation history. For instance, the original South Korean citation, *top right,* was donated by an Indianapolis resident.

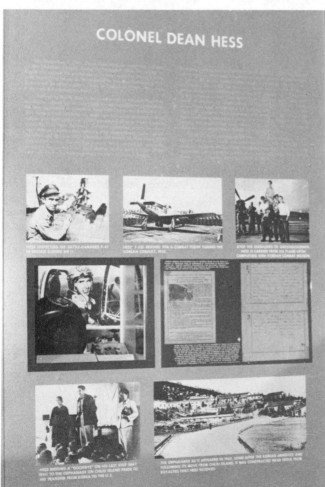

This exhibit recognizes the work of a former Ohio minister who served as a fighter pilot in World War II and Korea. However, Colonel Dean Hess is best noted for arranging an airlift to rescue thousands of Korean orphans from Communist armies sweeping in from the north. His "Operation Kiddy Car" flew the youngsters to safety on Cheju Island where he established an orphanage.

123

The North American F-100 Super Sabre made its combat debut during the Vietnam conflict. On October 29, 1953, it set the first faster-than-sound official world record of 755.1 miles per hour, becoming the world's first operational aircraft known to be capable of supersonic speeds in level or climbing flight. This F-100D, used by the Thunderbirds in 1964-68, is now featured in the Modern Flight Gallery.

Another sleek Super Sabre is displayed in the Air Power Gallery. As the aircraft's name implies, it evolved from the F-86 Sabre. New manufacturing techniques had to be developed to meet the increased speed and structural requirements of the Super Sabre, the first of the "century-series" aircraft. The F-100C, which made its first flight in 1955, featured such advances as an in-flight refueling system (note probe on wing) and an improved electronic bombing system. This Super Sabre, seen front and rear, was named and christened *Susan Constant* by Lady Churchill, wife of Sir Winston Churchill, in London on May 12, 1957.

A flattened nose is the hallmark of the RF-101, shown here landing at Tan Son Nhut Air Base in South Vietnam. This reconnaissance version took low-altitude photographs of Soviet missile sites during the 1962 Cuban crisis and of enemy activities during the late 1960s in Southeast Asia. *U.S. Air Force photo.*

McDonnell Aircraft Corporation built nearly 800 F-101 Voodoos with this distinctive tail between 1954 and 1961. The version most used was the pictured F-101B interceptor, which carried a pilot and a radar operator. A much different role was assigned this Voodoo. From 1960 to 1970 it was stationed at Wright-Patterson Air Force Base and used extensively for ejection-seat testing.

The Convair F-102A Delta Dagger on display was one of the first Air Force planes to intercept and convoy a Russian TU-20 Bear long-range bomber over the Arctic. At the time it served with a fighter-interceptor squadron in Iceland. A Ryan Firebee drone, used for target practice, appears to be attacking the F-102A. This Firebee set a record of twenty-five flights from 1958 to 1960. The radio-controlled drone deployed its own parachute after each mission so that it could be reused.

This photograph was taken during the September 1968 NATO fleet exercises while the Russian Bear was being tracked near the coast of Iceland. Other Soviet aircraft intercepted by F-102s that year included the TU-16 Badger, TU-95 Bear, and M-4 Bison. *U.S. Air Force photo.*

Because of its high landing speed, the F-102A would release a parachute from the compartment above its exhaust section as a breaking device. The F-102 was the world's first supersonic all-weather jet interceptor.

Mannequins dressed as fire fighters in this life-size diorama go to the aid of the "Thud" pilot. This particular Republic F-105G Thunderchief is credited with downing three MiGs over Vietnam. It is painted as when Americans flew it from Korat Royal Thai Air Base in 1972-73. The "Thud" was developed as a supersonic tactical fighter-bomber to replace the F-84F during the 1950s.

This Convair F-106A Delta Dart, which was developed from the F-102 Delta Dagger, landed itself on a snow-covered field after the pilot had been forced to eject because of a malfunction. Such all-weather interceptors first flew on December 26, 1956 and became operational with the Air Defense Command in July 1959. *U.S. Air Force Photo.*

The North American F-107A made its initial flight on September 10, 1956 reaching Mach 1.03. It never went into production, losing out to the F-105 as the standard fighter-bomber for the Tactical Air Command. Shown displayed in the Annex.

Lockheed's F-104 Starfighter was the first aircraft to hold simultaneous world records for speed, altitude, and time-to-climb. The F-104C on display, beneath the wing of a Lockheed AC-130A Hercules, served with the U.S. Air Force in West Germany, Spain, Taiwan, Vietnam, Laos, and Thailand. In 1962 it won first place in the "William Tell" Fighter Weapons Meet.

Although it first flew in August 1955, use of the Lockheed U-2 was kept secret until May 1960 when a civilian-piloted U-2 was downed on a reconnaissance flight over Soviet territory. The one displayed in the Museum Annex, the last U-2A built, made 285 flights during the 1960s to gather data on clear air turbulence at high altitudes.

The only remaining Lockheed YF-12A, designed as a high-altitude Mach 3 advanced interceptor, was delivered to the Air Force Museum in November 1979. It was capable of sustained flight at more than 2,000 mph at altitudes above 80,000 feet, and was the predecessor of the SR-71 *Blackbird* strategic reconnaissance aircraft. The YF-12A was introduced in 1964. *U.S. Air Force photo*.

Hundreds of the Northrop F-5 Freedom Fighters have been procured by the Air Force for use by allied nations around the world. They resemble the supersonic T-38 trainer. An American squadron flew combat missions with the YF-5A in Southeast Asia in 1966/67 to evaluate its combat performance. The YF-5A displayed was retired to the museum in 1970. A C-119J is in the background.

In spite of its size, the Cessna YA-37A is not a toy. The aircraft on display alongside the B-36 is one of two YAT-37D models. It was retired to the museum in December 1964 and recalled to active duty in August 1966 for final design testing of the A-37 attack model, then urgently needed for close air support of ground troops in South Vietnam. It was retired for a second time in July 1970 as the YA-37A.

Visitors easily peer into the Cessna YA-37A, which was modified from the T-37B primary trainer to evaluate it as a counterinsurgency attack and reconnaissance aircraft. The museum's chapel display can be seen in the background, above, before it was moved to the Modern Flight Gallery.

The twin-engined Cessna has two primary models: the T-37 trainer, seen over calm waters, and the A-37 Dragonfly, shown heavily loaded on a mission over Southeast Asia. One of the Cessna's features is its ability to carry out a mission with only one engine operating.

U.S. Air Force photo.

Although the conflict in Southeast Asia erupted during the "Jet Age," the first airman to win a Medal of Honor for service there was a pilot who flew this propeller-driven Douglas A-1E Skyraider. Maj. Bernard F. Fisher received the award from President Johnson on January 19, 1967.

Artist: Harvey Kidder

On March 10, 1966, Major Fisher had rescued a fellow pilot shot down over south Vietnam in the midst of enemy troops. A year later the repaired Skyraider was returned to the United States for preservation at the museum. The rescued pilot flew it from California to Ohio.

This Cessna 0-2A served with the 20th Tactical Air Support Squadron at Da Nang Air Base in the late 1960s. It is one of 346 special "push-and-pull" Cessna 337 Skymasters that entered U.S. Air Force service in 1966 to replace the 0-1 in the forward air controller role in Vietnam. *U.S. Air Force photo.*

Cessna O-1G Bird Dogs were used in Vietnam as two-place observation aircraft. Rockets were launched from the wing pods to mark enemy ground positions for other aircraft to strike. *U.S. Air Force photo.*

U.S. Air Force photo.

Designed as a replacement for the T-6 trainer, the North American T-28 Trojan went into production in 1950. Nearly 2,000 had been built when production ended in 1957. In 1962, the Air Force began modifying more than 200 T-28s as tactical fighter-bombers for counterinsurgency warfare in Vietnam. Those were redesignated the T-28D Nomad. A T-28A Trojan is displayed.

Designed to meet a Navy requirement, the Grumman HU-16 Albatross was able to operate from land or water and, with skis, from snow and ice. The prototype first flew on October 24, 1947, and was known as the SA-16A. During the Korean conflict the Albatross rescued nearly 1,000 United Nations personnel from coastal waters and rivers. The HU-16B on display was the last operational USAF Albatross. Two weeks before it was flown to the museum, it set a world altitude record for twin-engine amphibians when it reached 32,883 feet on July 4, 1973. Overhead is a Douglas O-46A.

An HU-16 on a search and rescue flight over Labrador in 1967. *U.S. Air Force photo.*

Several hundred downed fliers were rescued during World War II by crews flying the Consolidated OA-10 Catalina, the Army Air Force's version of the Navy PBY series seaplanes and amphibians. This aircraft was flown extensively by the Brazilian Air Force until 1981 in humanitarian roles in the Amazon Basin. It was flown to the museum three years later. *U.S. Air Force photo.*

The Sikorsky H-5 helicopter gained its greatest fame during the Korean conflict when it repeatedly rescued United Nations pilots from behind enemy lines. Displayed is one of the twenty-six YH-5As ordered in 1944. More than 300 of the various models were built by 1951.

Several fragile-appearing helicopters hang from the ceiling of the museum's large bay. This is the McDonnel XH-20 Little Henry, the world's first ram-jet helicopter, which flew in 1947/48. The jets are located on the ends of two rotor blades.

In addition to serving with the Air Force, the Vertol H-21 Workhorse was supplied to the U.S. Army, the French navy, the Royal Canadian Air Force, and the West German air force. The "Flying Banana" made its first flight in April 1952 and could carry twenty fully equipped troops or twelve litter patients. Displayed is a CH-21B.

One of President Eisenhower's original two helicopters is on display at the museum. He became the first U.S. President to fly in a heli-copter when an Air Force Bell UH-13J Sioux, a sister ship of the Sioux on display, carried him from the White House lawn on July 13, 1957.

Bensen's X-25A Gyrocopter was tested in 1968/69 as a means for downed flyers to escape from enemy territory.

KAMAN HH-43B "HUSKIE"

The "Huskie" was used primarily for aircraft crash rescue and fire-fighting. Delivery of the first H-43As to the USAF began in November 1958 for assignment to Tactical Air Command bases. Delivery of the -B series began in June 1959; it had better performance and could lift a greater load. (In mid-1962, the USAF changed the H-43 designa-tion to HH-43 to reflect the aircraft's rescue role.) HH-43Fs (the final USAF version) were used in Southeast Asia as "aerial fire trucks" and for rescuing downed airmen in both North and South Vietnam.

A Huskie on rescue alert could be airborne in approxi-mately one minute. It carried two rescuemen/fire-fighters in its cabin and a fire suppression kit hanging beneath it. Foam from the kit plus the powerful downwash of air from the rotors was used to open a path to crash victims.

The HH-43B on display, one of approximately 175 -Bs purchased by the USAF, established seven world records in 1961-1962 for helicopters in its class for rate of climb, altitude, and distance traveled. It was assigned to rescue duty with Detachment 3, 42nd Aerospace Rescue and Recovery Squadron, Kirtland AFB, N. Mex. prior to its retirement and flight to the museum in April 1973.

SPECIFICATIONS

Rotor diameter	47 ft.
Overall length	47 ft.
Height	17 ft. 2 in.
Weight	9,150 lbs. loaded
Armament	none
Engine	Lycoming T-53 of 860 hp.

PERFORMANCE

Maximum speed	120 mph
Cruising speed	105 mph
Range	185 miles
Service ceiling	25,000 ft.
Cost	$304,000

It was first flown in 1949, but the Sikorsky H-19 saw service for several decades in the United States and overseas. For instance, it was used for rescue missions during the Korean Conflict and for search missions off of West New Guinea in 1962 for the United Nations. *U.S. Air Force photo.*

After building 211 T-39 Sabreliners and variants for the U.S. Air Force and Navy, North American entered them in the commercial market as a highly successful executive jet transport. This T-39A was assigned to Bergstrom Air Force Base, Texas, from 1968 to 1973 in support of President Johnson. It was flown to the museum in 1984. *U.S. Air Force photo.*

Visitors at the Air Force Museum get a close look into the cockpit of this Fairchild Republic A-10 Thunderbolt II tank killer. It can fly 150 miles, remain on station for an hour, and then return home. More than 710 had been built when production ended in March 1984. Laser target-designation pods are standard equipment on active-duty models.

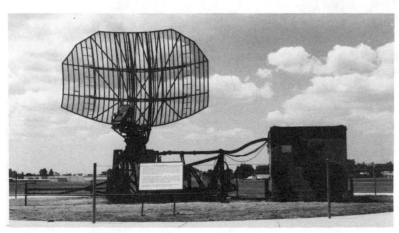

The AN/TPS-44A Radar set is an air-surveillance command and control radar that is used to locate and identify airborne targets. Radar sets of this type controlled tactical aircraft on close air-support missions in Southeast Asia during the 1960s. The fanlike antenna is foldable and the entire set is easily transportable.

During the 1960s, McDonnell Douglas F-4s set numerous speed, time-to-climb, and altitude records. The Phantom II carries a crew of two and three times the normal bomb load of a World War II B-17. It was flown by the Air Force in Vietnam on interception, close air support, and bombing missions. The airframe on display was used as a test bed for the fly-by-wire concept, employing electrical rather than mechanical interconnections between the pilot and control surfaces.

The McDonnell Douglas F-15A Eagle was the first U.S. fighter to have engine thrust greater than the normal weight of the aircraft, allowing it to accelerate while in a vertical climb. The single-seat F-15A on display, nicknamed "Streak Eagle," broke eight time-to-climb records between January 16 and February 1, 1975. During one such effort it reached an altitude of 98,425 feet in only 3 minutes and 27.8 seconds after releasing its brakes on the ground. Then it "coasted" to nearly 103,000 feet before descending.

General Dynamics built more than 500 versions of the F-111 before production ended in 1976. This A model, which was used against North Vietnamese forces, is one of 141 built. Similar Mach 2.5 tactical bombers were used in early 1991 during Operation Desert Storm against Iraq.
U.S. Air Force photo.

One of Lockheed's first F-117A Stealth fighters was delivered to the museum in July 1991 with thousands of spectators on hand for close-up views of the once-secret aircraft. The museum's Stealth is a full-scale development model similar to operational craft used against Iraqi forces. During Operation Desert Storm, F-117As flew about 2.5 percent of the combat sorties, but hit more than 30 percent of the strategic targets without receiving combat damage. *U.S. Air Force photo.*

MIKOYAN-GUREVICH MIG-15 "FAGOT"

The MiG-15 was developed by the Soviet Union following WW II. It began appearing in service in 1949, and by 1952 it had been provided to various Communist satellite nations, including North Korea where it was used extensively against United Nations forces.

The airplane on display was flown to South Korea on September 21, 1953 by a defecting North Korean pilot who was given a reward of $100,000. The airplane was subsequently flight-tested on Okinawa and then brought to Wright-Patterson AFB for additional flight tests. An offer by the U.S. to return the airplane to its "rightful owners" was ignored and in November 1957, it was transferred to the Air Force Museum for public exhibition.

SPECIFICATIONS

Span	33 ft. 1-1/2 in.
Length	36 ft. 4 in.
Height	11 ft. 2 in.
Weight	11,270 lbs. loaded.
Armament	Two 23mm cannon and one 37mm cannon, plus 2,000 lbs. of bombs or rockets.
Engine	VK-1 of 6,000 lbs. thrust (copy of British Rolls-Royce "Nene" engine).

PERFORMANCE

Maximum speed	670 mph.
Cruising speed	525 mph.
Range	500 miles.
Service ceiling	51,000 ft.

Soviet-designed MiG-21 Fishbeds have been flown by some 30 air forces around the world. This fighter was acquired by the Air Force Museum in 1989 through a trade with an entrepreneur who had purchased it in Romania. The MiG-21 probably had been built in Czechoslovakia. A MiG-17 also displayed at the museum was obtained from Egypt. A Boeing B-47 is in the background.

Based on the principle of the nineteenth-century Gatling gun, the T171 Vulcan cannon can fire 100 rounds per second as compared with the .50 caliber machine gun of World War II which fired only 14 rounds per second. The Vulcan 20 mm cannon was used in such USAF aircraft as the F-4, F-104, F-105 and B-58.

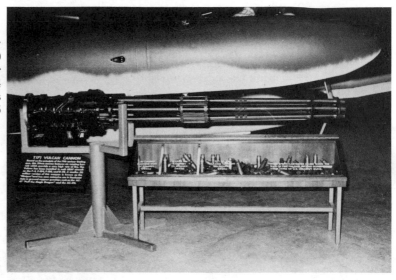

The Hughes AGM-65A Maverick rests beneath the duo jet engines of the B-36. The Maverick became the Air Force's primary air-to-ground guided missile in 1973. A rocket-propelled tactical missile, it is "locked on" to a target before launch and guides itself with a self-contained television guidance system. The AGM-65A can be launched from locations out of range of most ground defenses, thus decreasing chances of the launching aircraft being shot at. Mavericks are carried by the A-7D, F-4D, F-4E, and the A-10.

The Fairchild C-119 was designed to carry cargo, people, litter patients, and mechanized equipment. The Flying Boxcar has been in continual use since its first flight in 1947. The C-119J Packet on display has a unique history. It was especially modified for the midair retrieval of space capsules returning from orbit. On August 19, 1960, it made the world's first midair recovery of a space capsule when it snagged the Discoverer XIV parachute at 8,000 feet about 360 miles southwest of Honolulu.

Flying Boxcars saw much action during the Korean conflict as transports and returned to combat during the Vietnam conflict as AC-119 gunships in a ground support role. *U.S. Air Force photo.*

No, it's not W. C. Fields; it's the nose of a Douglas C-133A Cargo Master. Turboprop C-133s fulfilled the Air Force requirements for large capacity cargo aircraft throughout the 1960s. With its rear- and side-loading doors it was capable of handling a wide variety of military cargo. Most significant was its ability to transport ballistic missiles cheaper and faster than by trailer over highways.

The C-133A on display set a world record for propeller-driven aircraft on December 16, 1958, when it carried a payload of 117,900 pounds.

At the time of the 1954 French defeat in Southeast Asia, representatives of the major powers and of the Indochinese people met in Geneva and divided Indo-China into North Vietnam and South Vietnam, creating Laos and Cambodia at the same time. This section of the museum presents a part of the unsuccessful American attempt to keep South Vietnam free. The bulk of the U.S. Air Force combat support was flown from bases in Thailand, as indicated on the map.

This display contains the effects of Airman First Class William H. Pitsenbarger, who was killed in April 1966 while defending wounded comrades. He became the first enlisted man to be awarded the Air Force Cross, which ranks next to the Medal of Honor.

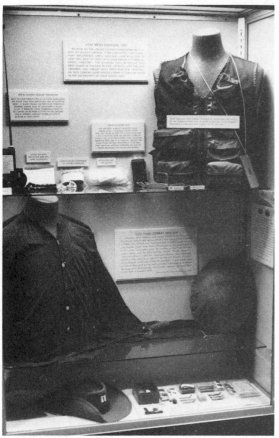

It was absolutely necessary for aircrewmen to carry jungle survival gear. This type of mesh survival vest included a two-way radio (*left*), strobe signaling light, nylon gill net for fishing, and a camouflaged tourniquet to control bleeding.

Aircraft used in Vietnam ranged from the large B-52 bomber (*left*), which operated from bases in Thailand and Guam, to the small 0-1 and 0-2 forward aircontroller aircraft that flew in Vietnam. The camouflage-painted projectile was dropped along jungle roads to monitor enemy truck and troop movements.

Visitors in the Modern Flight Gallery may inspect the interior of this Douglas C-124C, one of 448 Globemaster IIs built from 1949 to 1955. Museum visitors also are able to walk through a B-29 bomber from World War II and sit in the cockpit of an F-4 fighter representative of U.S. aircraft used over North Vietnam and Iraq. *U.S. Air Force photo.*

An Army utility aircraft is unloaded through the "clamshell" doors of a Globemaster in 1965 at Bien Hoa Air Base in Vietnam. *Old Shakey,* as it was affectionately known, also could carry tanks, field guns, trucks, bulldozers, helicopters, or two hundred fully-equipped soldiers. The C-124 fleet was retired in mid-1974. *U.S. Air Force photo.*

De Havilland Aircraft of Canada built the C-7A Caribou as a short takeoff and landing (STOL) utility transport, first flown in 1958. In Vietnam, its STOL capability made it particularly suitable for delivering troops, supplies, and equipment to isolated outposts. It could carry more than three tons. This combat veteran later served with the Air Force Reserve and was flown to the museum in May 1983. *U.S. Air Force photo.*

Members of the New York Air National Guard flew cargo in 1966 to Tan Son Nhut Air Base in Vietnam aboard this C-97. Most of the Stratofreighters were retired in 1973. *U.S. Air Force photo.*

Aircraft designers modified the Boeing B-29's belly and produced a transport they designated the C-97. The first of the seventy-four Stratofreighters flew in November 1944. A tanker version was introduced in 1950 with 816 eventually being built. This KC-97L was christened *Zeppel inheim* in 1973 by a mayor of the German town, honoring its use by the Ohio National Guard during the aerial refueling of NATO forces in Europe.

The first Lockheed C-130 Hercules flew in August 1954. They were still being constructed in the late 1970s for use around the world by many nations. With the U.S. Air Force they have been equipped for midair space capsule recover, ambulance service, drone launching, midair refueling of helicopters, reconnaissance, and radar weather mapping, as well as transports and gunships. This "A" model also was a test bed for numerous projects of the Air Force Systems Command.

Five Chance Vought XC-142s were built and only this one remains. The first of these unusual aircraft, which can fly straight up and down as well as forward, flew conventionally in late 1964. Vertical flight was achieved in January 1965, when the wings and engines were pointed skyward while the fuselage remained horizontal. The wings and engines were then tilted forward to attain horizontal flight. The four turbo-prop engines were linked together in such a way that one operating engine would turn all four propellers as well as the tail rotor. *U.S. Air Force photo.*

Four adjustable exhaust nozzles beneath the wing roots of the Hawker Siddeley XV-6A Kestrel could be rotated to provide thrust for vertical, backward, or hovering flight, as well as conventional forward movement. The United States received six of these aircraft for testing. When this Kestrel was flown to the musuem from Edwards Air Force Base, California, in 1970 it became the first aircraft to be airlifted by the giant C-5A.

The massive radomes above and below the fuselage of Lockheed's EC-121 Constellation carry six tons of electronic gear. On October 24, 1967, over the Gulf of Tonkin, this unarmed plane guided a United States fighter by radar into position to destroy an enemy MiG-21. This was the first time a weapons controller aboard an airborne radar aircraft had ever directed a successful attack on an enemy plane. The EC-121D on display was nicknamed *Triple Nickel* because of its serial number.

Constellations over Southeast Asia also directed fighter-bombers to their aerial refueling tankers and guided rescue planes to downed pilots. EC-121s, such as this one shown over Thailand, evolved from the Lockheed commercial transport and from the USAF version that flew radar patrol off the United States coasts. *U. S. Air Force photo.*

President Eisenhower used this VC-121E Constellation as his personal airplane between 1954 and 1961. His wife christened it *Columbine III* in honor of the official flower of Colorado, her home state. The interior has been configured so that visitors may walk through the aircraft.

A B-29 fuselage has been prepared for museum visitors to walk through. One is able both to view and touch crew areas, such as the panel here, as well as bomb casings. This fuselage is painted in the markings of the *Command Decision* whose crew shot down five MiG-15s during the Korean conflict.

As the visitor aboard the Superfortress walks through the bomb bay, he can see a portion of the museum's space exhibit.

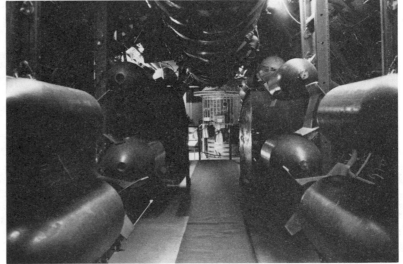

This Convair B-36J made the last flight ever made by a Peacemaker and was the first aircraft placed inside the museum. Because of its size, the B-36 had to be moved into the museum before construction was completed. The fuselage rests along the center line of the large bay while its wing tips reach to within a few feet of the arched walls. The B-36 intercontinental bomber was on duty as a deterrent to aggression from June 1948 until it was replaced by the B-52 in 1959.

This type of thermonuclear bomb was carried by B-36 bombers from 1954 to 1957. The Mark 17 weapon is nearly 25 feet long and weighed 41,400 pounds. A B-36 is shown in flight at right.

U.S. Air Force pho

When the B-36 was designed during World War II, landing gears with huge single wheels were envisioned. As the design was perfected, the single wheels were replaced by four smaller wheels which better distributed the weight of the aircraft on the runway. Loaded, the Peacemaker weighed about 410,000 pounds.

Protection for the B-36 bomber was the mission of the little McDonnell XF-85 Goblin, seen next to its mother ship and alone. It was to have been carried inside the B-36 and then launched from a trapeze to fight attackers with its four .50-caliber machine guns. Afterward it would fly under the bomber, attach itself to the trapeze, fold its wings, and be lifted back into the bomb bay. Although the Goblin was flown successfully, the project was canceled when midair refueling of fighter aircraft began to show greater promise. The Goblin first flew in August 1948 and was transferred to the museum two years later.

The North American B-45 Tornado was the first American four-engine jet bomber to fly and the first Air Force jet bomber to go into production. Work on the design began during World War II. B-45s were in use from 1948 to 1958, with some flying combat during the Korean conflict. A B-45C is pictured.

The Boeing B-47 Stratojet is the world's first swept-wing bomber. It also is the first airplane built solely for the delivery of nuclear weapons. In December 1953 it set a new transatlantic speed record averaging 650.5 miles per hour. The B-47E on display was the first Air Force aircraft to incorporate a "fly-by-wire" primary flight control system in which the pilot's command controls were transmitted to the control surfaces by electrical wires rather than by cables and mechanical linkages.

Lucky Lady II was the name of the first airplane to fly nonstop around the world. It was a Boeing B-50 Superfortress and the 23,452 mile trip required four aerial refuelings. The B-50 was the last propeller-driven bomber to be delivered to the Air Force. Originally called the B-29D, it had more powerful engines, a taller rudder, which could be lowered to the side for maintenance, a new wing structure, a new undercarriage, and hydraulic nosewheel steering. A WB-50D is on exhibition.

The KB-50J was converted from a bomber to a tanker by adding a jet engine and a fuel tank to each wing as well as modifying the tail to accommodate refueling equipment. This KB-50J has been at the museum since 1956.

Captured Communist soldiers described the Boeing B-52 Stratofortress *(center)* as the most feared weapons system used in the Vietnam conflict. In 1957, three B-52s set the first nonstop jet flight record around the world in 45 hours, 19 minutes. Fifteen years later the B-52 was playing an active role in Southeast Asia, flying daily bombing missions. The B-52G and H have an unrefueled range of more than 10,000 miles. By using aerial refueling its range is limited only by the endurance of its six-man crew. Exhibited is a B-52D that flew four bombing missions over North Vietnam in December 1972 and thus helped to free American prisoners of war during a massive demonstration of U.S. resolve by President Nixon. Nearly 20 years later, B-52 veterans of Vietnam were used to hasten the Iraqi defeat during Operation Desert Storm. *U.S. Air Force photo.*

Aerial refueling by the Boeing KC-135 Stratotanker has given the B-52 its around-the-world capability.
U.S. Air Force photo.

Great Britain developed this airplane and the United States borrowed its design, calling it the Martin B-57 Canberra. It served with the Tactical Air Command starting in 1954 and found a new lease on life in Vietnam as a low-level bomber and fighter.

U.S. Air Force photo.

U.S. Air Force photo.

The B-66 was the last tactical bomber built for the Air Force, and only the B-66B was designed exclusively as a bomber. Others served as tactical reconnaissance aircraft, while the final version, the WB-66D, was designed for electronic weather "recon." The Douglas RB-66D Destroyer on display flew combat missions in Southeast Asia in an electronic countermeasures role.

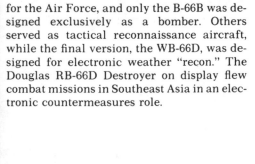

U.S. Air Force photo.

The Air Force's first supersonic operational bomber was the delta-wing Convair B-58 Hustler. The plane's wasp-waist fuselage left no room for bombs so a droppable two-component pod was carried beneath it. The pod contained extra fuel and a nuclear weapon, reconnaissance equipment, or other specialized gear. The B-58A at the museum set three separate speed records and earned the crew the Bendix and Mackay trophies for 1962 during a flight from Los Angeles to New York.

Prior to 1988 as visitors arrived at the museum area, one of the first individual planes they saw was the North American XB-70 Valkyrie thrusting out toward them looking for all the world like an oversized platypus. The XB-70 was designed to make use of a little-known phenomenon called "compression lift." This lift is achieved when the shock wave generated by the shape of an aircraft flying at supersonic speeds actually supports part of the airplane's weight. Built largely of stainless-steel honeycomb sandwich panels and titanium, the Valkyrie could drop its wing tips as much as 65 degrees at supersonic speeds to improve its stability. This XB-70 is the last of the two that operated from 1964 to 1969. Most aircraft in the background and the XB-70 were moved indoors when the Modern Flight Gallery was completed.

U.S. Air Force photo.

Northrop's Gee Whizz Deceleration Sled accelerated to 200 miles per hour along a 2,000-foot track, then stopped in 45 feet. The sudden stop developed deceleration forces such as those encountered in airplane crashes and the opening of parachutes. The tests were begun in 1947 for the Aeromedical Laboratory at Wright Field.

Bell designed and built six airplanes in the X-1 series, the last of which is the X-1B displayed at the museum. This flying laboratory was equipped with 1,-000 pounds of complex instruments to answer questions about the then strange new world of the sound barrier. Capt. Charles E. Yeager broke the sound barrier in an earlier model in a straight and level flight on October 14, 1947. Six years later he flew the X-1B to a record 1,650 miles per hour.

Douglas made only one X-3 Stiletto. It was designed to test aircraft features at supersonic speeds and high altitudes. Data gained from the X-3 program of the mid-1950s was of great value in the development of the F-104, X-15, and other high-performance aircraft. Two of the minihelicopters displayed behind the X-3 were self-propelled. The Nazi observation helicopter in the center was towed behind a submarine.

Mercury, Gemini, and Apollo space projects received significant contributions from the X-15 flight program. Several X-15 pilots earned astronaut ratings by flying above fifty miles and into the lower edges of space. The three North American X-15s which were built made 199 flights between 1959 and 1968. The X-15A-2 displayed set an unofficial world speed record of 4,520 miles per hour in August 1966.

U.S. Air Force Photo.

A tail view offers a sharp contrast between the X-3 (*left*) and the X-15. The Stiletto was powered by two jet engines with nearly 5,000 pounds of thrust combined, while the X-15 was powered by a rocket engine with over 50,000 pounds of thrust.

★ 7 | *Missiles and Space*

As visitors conclude their chronological walk through aviation history in the Air Power Gallery at the Air Force Museum, the last area they might visit features the exploration of space. Here, in the Space Gallery, they can see gondolas which, suspended from balloons, ascended to new heights; an actual capsule that carried Americans into space; samples of food eaten by American astronauts; gold-plated equipment recovered from early space tests; and full-scale satellites hanging dramatically overhead. Visitors can also hear and see Ohioan Neil A. Armstrong, via a brief museum movie, tell of carrying a piece of the original 1903 Wright Flyer to the moon. In a specially protected area, the visitors can see an actual moon rock.

Outdoors are displayed the giant space missiles that have helped protect the country and support the nation's peaceful exploration of space. Smaller missiles, which preceded man's venture into space, are also displayed outdoors, as well as in both the World War I and II exhibition areas. The famous X-15 rocket ship is indoors, too, in the Modern Flight Gallery.

When the Air Force launched its first satellite in 1958, it took the lead in developing space systems to improve national security. As the Department of Defense's principal space agency, the Air Force supports the Army, Navy, and the National Aeronautics and Space Administration. Approximately two-thirds of the payloads placed in earth, sun, or moon orbit by the United States in the early decades were launched by the Air Force. While developing space technology for the future, the Air Force and the nation's space program have developed technology for today. Weather and communications satellites have more than proven their worth. And satellites have become nearly indispensable for surveillance, warning, mapping, education, and ecology manage-

154

ment. In fact, many thousands of new products and techniques have resulted from space and missile development. These have proven useful to both military and civilian consumers. Only one such item is the tiny, long-life battery used to power electric wristwatches.

A family examines a moon rock brought to Earth in 1972. In the Kitty Hawk panel are fragments of the 1903 Wright Flyer that Neil Armstrong took to the moon in 1969. Overhead, in the adjoining Vietnam display, is a Cessna 0-2 that has a service ceiling of 19,300 feet.

Visions of space travel can be conjured up by visitors in this section of the Space Gallery. In fact, the Apollo 15 Falcon command module *(right)* took three Air Force astronauts to the moon in 1971 on a twelve-day mission. Maj. Alfred M. Worden, Jr. remained in the capsule in moon orbit while Col. David R. Scott and Lt. Col. James B. Irwin explored the moon. The development of space suits is depicted on the left.

This Manhigh II balloon gondola was used in a project established in December 1955 to obtain scientific data on the behavior of man in an environment above 99 percent of the earth's atmosphere, and to investigate cosmic rays and their effects upon man. Three balloon flights to the edge of space were made during the program.

Project Stargazer was established in January 1959 for high-altitude astronomical investigation from above ninety-five percent of the earth's atmosphere. This permitted undistorted visual and photographic observations of the stars and planets. On December 13/14, 1962, Capt. Joseph Kittinger and Mr. William White made a balloon flight to an altitude of 82,200 feet over New Mexico in a Stargazer gondola. The flight also provided valuable information concerning the development of pressure suits and associated life support systems.

Captain Joseph Kittinger also ascended alone to an altitude of 102,800 feet in an Excelsior open gondola in August 1962. He set two balloon ascension records on the way up and two parachute records on the way down. He later served as a fighter-bomber pilot in Southeast Asia, was captured by the North Vietnamese, and was freed during "Operation Homecoming" in 1973.

CAPT. KITTINGER IN GONDOLA DURING LAUNCH FROM HOLLOMAN AFB N. MEX.

PHOTO OF CAPT. KITTINGER BY AUTOMATIC CAMERA AS HE PREPARED TO JUMP FROM 102,800 FEET

FALLING PRIOR TO DEPLOYMENT OF STABILIZING CHUTE

LANDING ON THE RUGGED NEW MEXICO DESERT

Two Philippine monkeys and two white mice were launched to an altitude of 36 miles on May 22, 1962, to help man prepare for his journeys into space. They traveled skyward at 2,000 miles per hour aboard an Aerojet Aerobee rocket and returned safely to earth in its nose section dangling beneath a parachute.

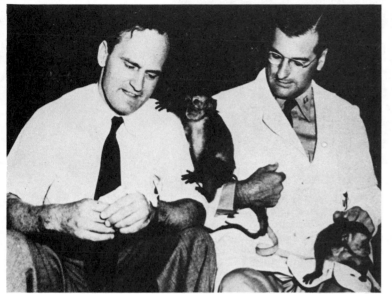

Monkeys Patricia and Mike thus became the first primates to reach so high an altitude. The white mice, Mildred and Albert, romp on the hands of the gentleman in the white shirt. Their flight provided invaluable data for the survival of man during rocket launch as well as man's existence in the weightless environment of space.

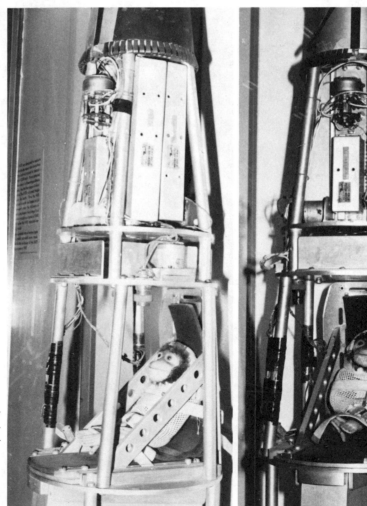

A monkey doll illustrates in two views how Patricia traveled while aboard the Aerobee. Mike rode in a lower compartment—on his back.

This Lockheed Research Satellite Engineering Development Model was designed to carry several types of scientific payloads in order to make it more versatile in investigating space. Maximum weight at launch was 350 pounds. The first launch of this type satellite was in 1963 from an Agena space vehicle already orbiting the earth. During hundreds of orbits, the satellite radioed back 100,000,000 measurements of scientific data.

Closeup of Northrop OV-2-5 space satellite.

Space Shuttle operations stimulated the need for such equipment as this extravehicular activity "E-V-A" unit to repair items in space. The backpack originally was designed for the Gemini program. *U.S. Air Force photo.*

This array of missiles faces the museum. The four units in the foreground are (*left to right*) the Northrop SM-62 Snark, Martin CGM-13B Mace, Martin TM-61A Matador, and the Boeing CIM-10A Bomarc. The Snark and the vertical missiles (*background*) were capable of intercontinental ranges.

The nation's first intercontinental guided missile, the Northrop SM-62 Snark, was equipped with a self-contained and nonjammable guidance system. It was capable of directing the missile with unprecedented accuracy through all weather conditions to the designated target. The Snark was extremely mobile and could be airlifted to any site within a few hours. It was a difficult adversary for enemy defenses during the 1950s.

As a surface-to-surface missile, the Martin CGM-13 Mace was in operation from 1959 until the early 1970s. It used a guidance system that permitted a low-level attack by matching a radar return with radar terrain maps.

MARTIN TM-61A "MATADOR"

The Matador was a surface tactical missile designed to carry either a conventional or a nuclear warhead. Originally designated as the B-61, the USAF's first "pilotless bomber," it was similar in concept to the WWII German V-1 "buzz bomb." The Matador was launched by a booster rocket from a mobile 40-foot trailer and was controlled electronically from the ground during flight. Immediately after launch, the booster rocket fell away and the missile continued on course to target powered by its jet engine.

Development of the Matador began in August 1945 and the XB-61 was first launched on January 19, 1949. Operational TM-61s which later followed were the first tactical guided missiles in the USAF inventory. The first Pilotless Bomber Squadron (Light) was organized in October 1951 for test and training purposes and in March 1954 the first Matador unit was deployed overseas to bolster NATO forces in West Germany. TM-61 units were also sent to Korea and Taiwan.

Martin delivered the 1,000th Matador in mid-1957, but in 1959 a phase-out of the Matador began in favor of a more advanced version, the Martin "Mace."

SPECIFICATIONS

Span . . . . 27 ft. 11 in.
Length . . . . 39 ft. 8 in.
Height . . . . 9 ft. 8 in.
Weight: 13,593 lbs. (at launch)
Armament . . Conventional or nuclear warhead
Engines: Allison J33 of 4,600 lbs. thrust; Aerojet solid-propellant booster rocket of 57,000 lbs. thrust

PERFORMANCE

Maximum speed . . . 600 mph (level flight); supersonic during final dive)
Range . . . . 690 miles
Service ceiling . . . . 44,000 ft.

Cost $132,000

Testing of the Boeing CIM-10 Bomarc began in 1952, became operational in 1960, and was phased out by 1972. It was a surface-launched pilotless interceptor, which was designed to destroy enemy aircraft. The "A" model shown here had a range of 260 miles. Improved "B" models were stationed in the United States and Canada.

Silent sentinels in front of the museum are these missiles (*left to right*): Boeing LGM-30G Minuteman III, Boeing LGM-30A Minuteman I, Chrysler PGM-19 Jupiter, Martin HGM-25A Titan I, Douglas PGM-16 Thor, and the Convair HGM-16F Atlas. A bicentennial time capsule is buried near the flagpole. It is to be opened in the year 2076.

A Minuteman is launched at sunset from Vandenberg Air Force Base, California. *U.S. Air Force photo*.

Research data for the development of an intercontinental winged missile was gathered by the North American X-10. Although thirteen of these supersonic vehicles were built and flown in the mid-1950s, only this one is known to exist. *U.S. Air Force photo*.

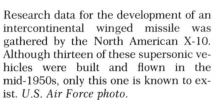

This type Aerojet rocket engine powers the second stage of the Minuteman 3 ICBM (intercontinental ballistic missile). After a Minuteman is launched by its larger first-stage engine, the first-stage section is jettisoned when its fuel is depleted, and the second-stage engine takes over to boost the missile higher and faster. It, likewise, is jettisoned, and the third-stage engine then takes over to propel the nuclear warhead onward toward its preselected enemy target.

The Chrysler PGM-19 Jupiter intermediate-range ballistic missile (IRBM) was developed by the Army's Ballistic Missile Agency under Dr. Wernher von Braun. When it became operational in 1959, it was placed under Air Force control. Originally designed as the SM-78, the Jupiter was a single-stage, liquid-propellant missile using an all-inertial guidance system. Jupiter squadrons of fifteen missiles each were deployed at NATO launch sites in Italy and Turkey in 1961. As more advanced missiles were developed, the Jupiter became outdated and in 1963 it was withdrawn from military use. Some Jupiters were used as first-stage boosters to launch space satellites.

Liquid propellants for the Martin HGM-25A Titan I's Aerojet rocket engines were kerosene fuel and liquid oxygen. The Titan I was the first Air Force ICBM to be placed in hardened underground silos for protection against enemy attack. However, they had to be lifted from their silos to the surface by elevator prior to launching. By 1965 Titan Is were being phased out in favor of Titan IIs, which offered greater range and payload and which were launched from within their silos.

A close-up of the Titan I engines which have a first-stage thrust of 300,000 pounds and a second-stage thrust of 80,000 pounds.

When the Minuteman I (*second from right*) became operational in 1962, it was nicknamed "the instant missile," in that it was constantly ready for immediate firing. It uses solid propellants, as does the Minuteman III (*right*), which was introduced in 1970. There are 1,000 such missiles on alert in the Central Plains states. Wright Brothers Hill is in the left background.

The Titan II gyroscope, which is preprogrammed by a computer installed in the missile, steers with such accuracy that it will pinpoint a target 10,000 miles from the launch site. The gyroscope is gold-plated because gold is the best-known material for withstanding corrosion and temperature changes encountered in space.

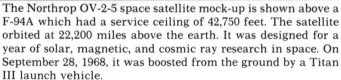

The Northrop OV-2-5 space satellite mock-up is shown above a F-94A which had a service ceiling of 42,750 feet. The satellite orbited at 22,200 miles above the earth. It was designed for a year of solar, magnetic, and cosmic ray research in space. On September 28, 1968, it was boosted from the ground by a Titan III launch vehicle.

The Douglas PGM-17 Thor missile entered active military service in September 1958, thus becoming the Free World's first operational IRBM (intermediate-range ballistic missile). With the development of more advanced missiles, the Thor was retired from its military role in 1963. However, some were modified and used extensively as launch vehicles for U. S. space research. As a military weapon it carried a nuclear warhead. The XB-70 is in the background.

The Discoverer XIV capsule on display was the first item to be ejected by a satellite orbiting in space and to be recovered in midair. It was launched August 18, 1960, by a Thor booster and propelled into orbit by an Agena. Upon descent and reentering the earth's atmosphere it released a parachute which was snagged by a C-119 recovery airplane. Discoverer XIV thus completed a 27-hour, 450,000-mile journey through space.

The Convair HGM-16F Atlas, the Free World's first ICBM, was designed to be launched at an enemy target at least 5,000 miles away. Lt. Col. John Glenn was put into orbit on February 20, 1962, by an Atlas missile. It also has been used to launch a variety of unmanned spacecraft including Ranger, Surveyor, and Mariner.

This is an Atlas ICBM being launched from Vandenberg Air
Force Base, California, in February 1962.

U.S. Air Force photo.

Artist: Russ Turner

General Bernard A. Schriever spearheaded the
development of the Air Force's early accomplishments in space. His portrait is part of the
Air Force Art Collection at the museum.

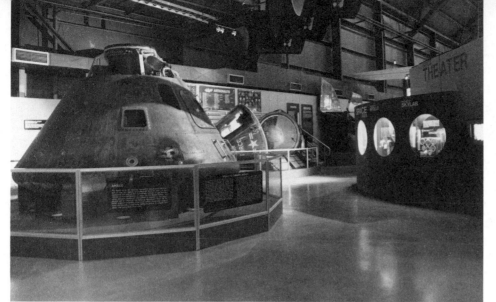

Renovated and enlarged in 1990-91, the Space Gallery here includes *(left to right)* the Apollo 15 command module, Gemini and Mercury spacecraft, tail of the X-24A, space foods display, and a space theater featuring the Project Apollo story narrated by Neil Armstrong. *U.S. Air Force photo.*

This type of space sled was once considered for travel near orbiting spacecraft. Eventually, a back-pack design was chosen for such extravehicular activity.

One man rode into space in this type of McDonnell Mercury spacecraft *(right)* during the six Project Mercury flights from 1961 to 1963. Although the McDonnell Gemini spacecraft *(left)* was six inches shorter, it was designed to carry two men into space. Ten manned Gemini missions were flown in 1965 and 1966 as the bridge to landing on the moon with the Apollo module. The Mercury on display was used to provide parts to support the flight of L. Gordon Cooper, Jr. on May 15-16, 1963 while the Gemini on display was used for thermal-qualification testing. *U.S. Air Force photo.*

Two lifting bodies, the Martin X-24A (not shown) and the X-24B (shown here), helped pave the way for the design and construction of the Space Shuttle, which was being tested in 1977. (A lifting body is an aircraft that derives lift from the shape of its fuselage rather than from wings. It is thus better able to cope with the heating associated with high speeds.) The two lifting bodies made sixty-four powered flights from the wing of a B-52 between March 1970 and November 1975. The program was managed by the Air Force Flight Dynamics Laboratory at Wright Field.

One Thiokol XLR-11 rocket engine of 8,000-pounds thrust and two Bell LLRV optional landing rockets of 400-pounds thrust each powered the X-24B. It had a maximum speed of 1,163 miles per hour.

The X-24A was modified into the X-24B in 1972 when the testing of the former was completed. The X-24A on display was built as the jet-powered SV-5J for flight traiing, but never flown. It was converted to the X-24A configuration for display purposes. *U.S. Air Force photo.*

★ 8 | *Special Exhibits*

Unique exhibits and many of the U.S. Air Force Museum's smaller displays are sometimes presented to the public in the two exhibit halls of the facility's core building. Some exhibits remain in those areas while others are later moved to close proximity with the aircraft or historical era to which they are related. At times the personalities associated with the display attend the unveiling ceremony.

When the Southeast Asia POW display was unveiled, for instance, two former prisoners of war participated. Both had undergone medical and administrative processing at Wright-Patterson AFB and both had contributed memorabilia which they had brought out of North Vietnam. One donned his former prison garb for a photograph which is included in the display. A large number of black airmen who had flown in World War II attended the program at which a display was dedicated in recognition of their contributions in all conflicts, beginning with the First World War. Much of this display was subsequently incorporated into other exhibits as they were expanded. And Civil Air Patrol members and leaders, past and present, were on hand when their display was unveiled. These and presentations of newly acquired aircraft are announced in advance through area news media so that interested persons may attend.

Permanent displays in the Hall of Honor and the Kettering Hall, in addition to those mentioned in Chapter 1, include authenticated pieces of the first Wright Flyer, drawings by Woodi Ishmael of Medal of Honor recipients, insignia cut from World War I airplanes, official insignia of major Air Force commands, recent accessions of note, the Eugene W. Kettering collection of model airplanes, the evolution of USAF aircraft markings, and samples of the Air Force Art Collection. The annual Student Aviation Art Show is hung in the Kettering Hall each spring as well.

The nation's highest military award, the Medal of Honor, has been presented to at least sixty-two airmen. This includes Special Congressional Medal Awards to Capt. Charles A. Lindbergh, Brig. Gen. William "Billy" Mitchell, Brig. Gen. Charles E. Yeager, and Lt. Gen. Ira C. Eaker. General Eaker received his award in 1979 on the seventy-sixth anniversary of powered flight. Normally, the Medal of Honor is awarded for "conspicuous gallantry and intrepidity at the risk of life above and beyond the call of duty." It was awarded to four Air Force men in World War I, thirty-eight in World War II, four in the Korean conflict, and twelve for combat in Southeast Asia. The distinctive Air Force design (*right*) was created in 1965. Maj. Bernard F. Fisher was the first to receive it on January 19, 1967.

Many of the museum's smaller displays are introduced to the public in the gallery that houses the Medal of Honor exhibit. Here in words and pictures is the story of "Aerial Photography and the Cuban Missile Crisis" of 1962. Supported by photographic evidence and a strong military force, President Kennedy persuaded the Soviet Union to withdraw its offensive missiles from Cuba.

Civil Air Patrol members flew thousands of hours in light airplanes such as this Piper L-4, searching for enemy submarines in coastal waters during World War II. This is the military version of the Piper J3 Cub, which was originally designated the O-59. During the war it also was used to direct artillery fire, train pilots, instruct glider pilots, and to perform courier service and frontline liaison.

The Civil Air Patrol was established on December 1, 1941, by decree of the Director of Civilian Defense Fiorella H. La Guardia. The CAP is an official auxiliary of the United States Air Force. As such, it carries out an education program for youth and assists with the search and rescue of downed airplanes, both military and civilian.

172

Over the decades, various Air Force and Air National Guard aerial teams have demonstrated the performance capabilities of operational aircraft and the skill of military pilots. This exhibit presents the history of the Thunderbirds and other aerial demonstrations teams back to the Air Corps' Three Musketeers of 1928.

At the request of numerous visitors in early 1991, museum employees assembled a temporary display of Operation Desert Storm munitions and guidance systems as the fighting was winding down in the Persian Gulf War. In the background are just two of the types of allied aircraft used against Iraqi forces, the B-52 bomber *(number 665)* and the F-5 Freedom Fighter at its side. *U.S. Air Force photo.*

Col. Bernt Balchen was America's greatest Arctic expert of modern times. The Norwegian native was the chief pilot in 1928–31 for Admiral Byrd's Antarctic Expedition and on November 29, 1929, Balchen piloted the first aircraft to fly over the South Pole. After serving in World War I, he was recalled to duty in 1948 and in the following year made the first nonstop flight over the Polar region from Alaska to Europe. Lowell Thomas dubbed him the "Last of the Vikings."

The history, traditions, and uniforms of the Air Force Academy are highlighted in this special exhibit. Located at Colorado Springs, the four-year institution produces new second lieutenants with college degrees.

A portion of the Air Force Art Collection (*foreground*) and the Kettering airplane model exhibit (*facing the sofas*) are shown in this gallery. Museum offices, restaurant, and additional displays are located upstairs.

A collection of approximately 600 aircraft models was presented to the Air Force Museum Foundation for permanent display by the late Eugene W. Kettering. Started in mid-1920s, this collection reflects the significant advancements of civilian and military aircraft of many nations. It is a capsule history of aviation in model form, 1-76th the size of the full-scale aircraft. The models are all handmade of balsa wood and were once displayed in the study of Mr. Kettering's home. On the wall is a 1908/1909 Wright brothers' propeller. The Kettering model collection occupies two walls, and historic memorabilia from Mr. Kettering's study are displayed in glass-covered tables.

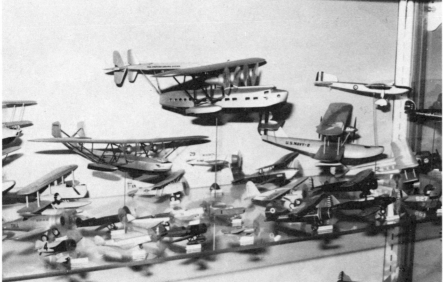

"I authenticate the above pieces as genuine parts of the original 'Kitty Hawk' plane, flown on December 17, 1903. They are from parts broken when the plane, while standing on the ground, was overturned by the wind after the fourth flight of the day." Signed: Orville Wright.

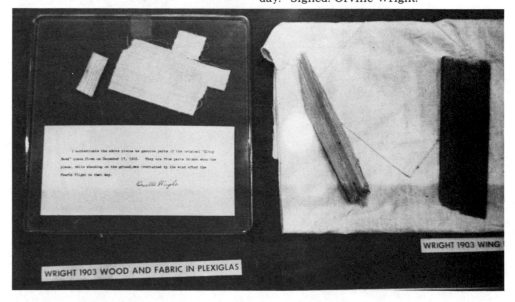

WRIGHT 1903 WOOD AND FABRIC IN PLEXIGLAS

WRIGHT 1903 WING

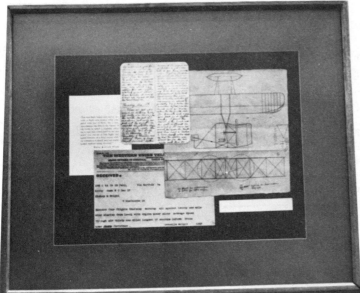

This picture hangs in the gallery containing the Kettering model airplanes. It is a collage of copies of Wilbur Wright's sketch of the first flying machine, the Wrights' flight log of December 17, 1903, and a telegram addressed to their father, Bishop M. Wright, 7 Hawthorne Street, Dayton, telling of their successful flight. An extract from the note (*top left*) gives the Wright brothers' definition of the flight of an aircraft powered by an engine: "A machine carrying a man raised itself by its own power into the air in free flight, had sailed forward on a level course without reduction of speed and had finally landed without being wrecked."

The Air Force Art Collection contains over 4,700 paintings, which are displayed worldwide. Nationally, there are permanent displays at the Smithsonian Institution, the Air Force Academy, and the Air Force Museum. The pictures, which are rotated from time to time, are in two categories: Historical, 1915 to 1953; and Contemporary, 1954 to the present.

Mark C. Sloan, "Mr. Air Force Museum"

Artist: Keith Meininger

Armed Forces Day at Tachikawa AFB, Japan

Artist: Ozni Brown

Clark Field, the Philippines

Artist: Earl Gross

Unloading a Conac Reserve C-119

Artist: Wesley B. McKeown

The New Look. Artist: Bill Edwards

Warming Up—Guam to Vietnam was painted on a board from a box which had contained bomb fuses. Some of the original lettering was purposely permitted to show through the paint by the artist, Howard Koslow.

Many members of the Society of Illustrators donate paintings and drawings to the Air Force Art Collection. Here two artists are shown gathering ideas at Ent Air Force Base.

Artists at Ent. Artist: Dale B. Gallon

During World War II the mighty Eighth Air Force could launch 3,000 combat aircraft on a single day. In October 1982 survivors and friends of the Eighth Air Force dedicated this monument to the unit's many achievements. The plaque beneath the propeller blade lists the names of seventeen members who earned the Medal of Honor. It also lists the number of other awards received, including 442,300 Air Medals and 7,033 Purple Hearts. The far side of the pylon has a map of southeast England, known as East Anglia, with the eighty airfields of the Eighth Air Force.

Comradeship between air and ground crews during World War II is depicted in this memorial dedicated at the museum in September 1980. It was commissioned by former members of the 92nd Bombardment Group, a B-17 unit of the Eighth Air Force also known as "Fame's Favored Few." H. Richard Duhme, Jr., of Washington University handled the sculpting.

Artist: Maxine McCaffrey

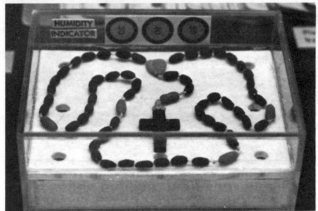

This rosary is typical of those made in North Vietnamese POW camps. It was secretively made in 1971 or 1972 by Navy Comdr. Paul Schultz and given to Air Force Col. John P. Flynn, who smuggled it from North Vietnam during the POW release program.

Many museum visitors are attracted to the Southeast Asia prisoner-of-war display of which this picture is a part. Several items were contributed by former POWs who received their medical and administrative processing during "Operation Homecoming" at Wright-Patterson Air Force Base.

Thirty former POWs were welcomed home by their families and friends at Wright-Patterson Air Force Base in the early months of 1973. The officer in the open doorway met his family at the next stop. *U.S. Air Force photo.*

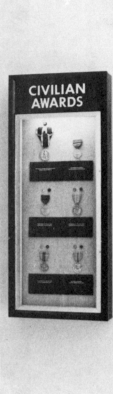

THIS TREE
IS A LIVING TRIBUTE TO
PRISONERS OF WAR AND
MISSING IN ACTION
IN SOUTHEAST ASIA
23 OCTOBER 1972
DONATED BY
VOLUNTEERS FOR POW/MIA

Recognition for bravery or for a "job well done" is given to civilians as well as active duty members of the Air Force. The lower half of the military display shows various unit insignia patches.

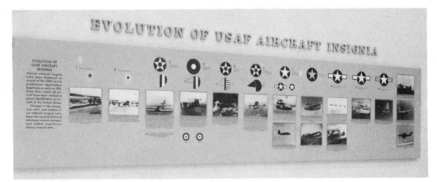

Changes in the design, size, color, and location of national insignia on Air Force aircraft have been the result of technical advances, mission changes, and combat experience. During World War II, for example, the red circle within the white star was removed to avoid confusion with the rising sun insignia of the Japanese.

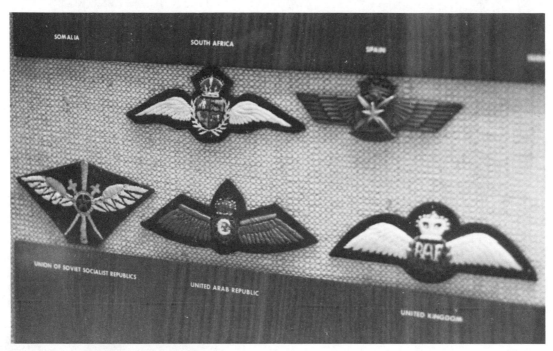

A few of the foreign wings displayed in a Wings of the World case are those from South Africa, Spain, Union of Soviet Socialist Republics, United Arab Republic, and the United Kingdom. A twin case not seen here features American wings and badges, past and present, including pilot's, navigator's, missileman's, flight surgeon's, nurse's, and parachutist's wings.

Humor has always been a part of the American experience, and so it is with Air Force life. Some of the lighter moments in the history of the nation's air arm are illustrated here.

A very important part of flying that the average person is not too concerned with is flying safety. This case displays several of the more humorous Blunder Trophies for safety violations. None of them is explained; however, the astute observer is able to conjure up several ideas.

Automobiles and airplanes have at least one key, common element. Both depend on spark plugs. This display is one of three. The others are spark plugs to 1940 and jet and rocket engine igniters. Prior to World War I most of the plugs used in the United States were made in Europe. When the famous B-36 was constructed, it was designed to fly at 45,000 feet, but it was limited to 30,000 feet until a new type spark plug was developed. While a spark plug works throughout a flight, jet and rocket engine igniters work only to start their engines.

Distinguished visitors from the Soviet Union presented this model of the Tupolev 134A to the museum in September, 1973.

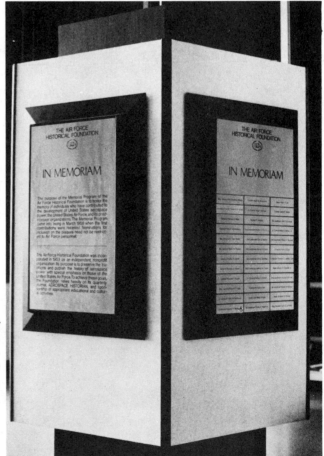

Individuals who have contributed to the development of United States areospace power and the Air Force are honored in this memorial of the Air Force Historical Foundation. Names range from General Orville Anderson to the Wright brothers.

"HIGH FLIGHT"

Oh! I have slipped the surly bonds of earth
And danced the skies on laughter-silvered wings;
Sunward I've climbed, and joined the tumbling mirth
Of sun-split clouds — and done a hundred things
You have not dreamed of — wheeled and soared and swung
High in the sunlit silence. Hov'ring there,
I've chased the shouting wind along, and flung
My eager craft through footless halls of air.
Up, up the long, delirious, burning blue
I've topped the wind-swept heights with easy grace
Where never lark, or even eagle flew —
And, while with silent lifting mind I've trod
The high untrespassed sanctity of space,
Put out my hand and touched the face of God.

John Gillespie Magee, Jr.

Contrary to popular belief, Pilot Officer John Gillespie Magee, Jr., did not write his celebrated poem "High Flight" on the back of an envelope. It was written on a standard piece of writing paper, which is included in this display beneath his portrait. Magee was an American who was born in Shanghai, China, and who was killed at the age of nineteen while flying with the Royal Canadian Air Force in December 1941 over England.

Many celebrities served in uniform during World War II. Those saluted on these panels are (*right to left*) President Ronald Reagan, James Stewart, Clark Gable, Gene Raymond, Jackie Coogan, and Joe Lewis.

Push a button and hear "High Flight" recited by the mother of John Gillespie Magee, Jr., and the Air Force song sung by its composer, Robert Crawford. The first page of his music was taken to the moon on July 20, 1971, aboard the Apollo 15 Falcon lunar module.

World War I Unit Insignia

WWI flyers were, in general, uniquely carefree and individualistic. For example, whenever one of them shot down an enemy airplane in his own territory, he would go to great extremes to visit the crash site and take a part of the vanquished airplane. Likewise, he often would save a piece of his own airplane in which he had been shot down, if he had been sufficiently fortunate to come down inside his own battle lines and survive the incident. He would even save the insigne from the airplane in which a buddy was killed. In short, he was a great "souvenir collector."

U.S. Air Service personnel were no exception. In fact, they often cut from the fuselages of their own airplanes the fabric on which their insignia had been painted, regardless of whether the plane was battle-damaged, being transferred to another squadron, or being sent to a rear depot for salvage. Interestingly, they ignored orders which had been issued to prevent such practice.

The insignia on display, 9 in each side hall, representing 18 of the 45 U.S. Air Service squadrons on the Front in France at the time of the Armistice, were cut from airplanes by U.S. Air Service men. All have been preservation-treated and are covered with special filtering glass to protect them from damaging ultraviolet rays.

Insignia of 138th Aero Squadron from Capt. Walter H. Schultze's Spad 7.

Insignia of 27th Aero Squadron from Lt. Frank Luke's Spad 13.

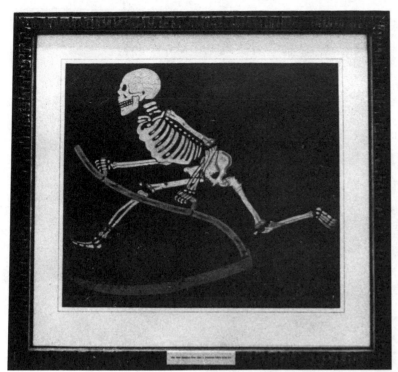

Insignia of 13th Aero Squadron from Capt. J. Dickinson Este's Spad 13.

Insignia of 141st Aero Squadron from Lt. Charles D'Olive's Spad 13.

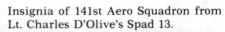

Insignia of 139th Aero Squadron from the Spad 13 flown by Lt. David Putnam in which he was shot down and killed on September 13, 1918, while going to the aid of Allied observation aircraft under attack by eight German planes.

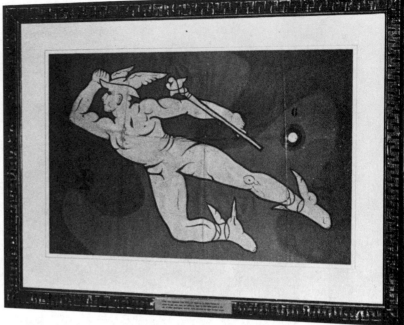

Insignia of 135th Aero Squadron from Lt. Howard E. Sproull's D. H. 4. The 135th was the first U.S. unit to use the American-built D.H. 4s.

Insignia of 91st Aero Squadron from Lt. Merle R. Husted's Salmson. (The photograph on the right shows the airplane upside down after a forced landing in heavy fog on December 6, 1918, with the Army of Occupation.)

COCKBURN-LANGE WORLD WAR I AERIAL COMBAT PHOTOGRAPHS

These twenty-one photographs (plus twenty-two out of view) compose one of the most complete sets of the famous Cockburn-Lange collection known to exist. They were donated to the museum in 1971 by Mr. Reed M. Chambers, a well-known World War I combat pilot with the 94th "Hat-in-the-ring" Squadron.

The Cockburn-Lange photographs have been the subject of controversy for years. They were said to have been taken by an unnamed Royal Air Force pilot using a camera removed from a downed German airplane. The collection was first shown at a New York aviation art show in 1931 and later appeared in an anonymously authored book titled *Death in the Air*. When examined by a number of experienced World War I pilots, the photographs produced reactions varying from positive belief in their authenticity to equally strong opinions that they were a hoax.

Research concluded in 1984 now seems to prove that the photographs were fabricated with model airplanes and clever studio work by Wesley D. Archer, an American who served with the Royal Flying Corps/Royal Air Force and who was, in fact, the author of *Death in the Air*. The photographs, genuine or not, were successfully used to illustrate the book and, in so doing, became widely known themselves.

The collection is exhibited because it has become a significant part of aviation lore. The photographs illustrate World War I aerial combat from the aviator's point of view, however distorted that view may have become with the passage of time. Museum officials leave it to the visitor to ponder the authenticity and merit of these photographs.

Insignia of 103rd Aero Squadron from Lt. Stewart E. Edgar's Spad 13.

Air Force people stationed at Wheelus Air Base paid for the stained-glass chapel window seen here. It commemorates the courage of the B-24 *Lady Be Good* crew who perished in the African desert in 1943. The window was brought to the United States when the U.S. Air Force vacated the Libyan base. Below are examples of Christian and Jewish chaplain traveling kits displayed at the sides of the window.

Chaplain uniforms from two World Wars and other memorabilia are included in the Air Force Chapel display originally on the second floor. It is now in the Modern Flight Gallery.

Seal of the first Chief of USAF Chaplains, Chaplain, Maj. Gen., Charles I. Carpenter. (Donated by Chaplain, Maj. Gen., Charles I. Carpenter, USAF, Ret., Milford, Dela.)

USAF CHAPLAINS

The official origin of the chaplaincy within the American military services was a resolution passed by the Continental Congress in 1775. Since that time, military chaplains have administered to the spiritual needs of the serviceman, often at the risk of their own lives. For example, during WW II 8,896 ministers, priests, and rabbis served as chaplains with American military forces. Of these, 78 were killed in action, four died in Japanese prison camps, and 264 were wounded in action. The chaplaincy of the U.S. Air Force was separated from that of the U.S. Army on June 11, 1948 with the creation of the Office of the Chief of Air Force Chaplains, almost a year after the USAF became a separate service.

Today there are more than 1,000 chaplains within the Air Force, whose role involves not only worship and pastoral functions, but also religious and moral education, personal counseling, humanitarian services, cultural leadership, and public relations. Whether it be at a base chapel near a major American city or before an altar made of snow blocks north of the Arctic Circle, the chaplain brings solace to the lives of servicemen and women wherever they may serve.

Protestant cross used in Chapel No. 1 at Randolph AFB, Texas from 1936 until 1972. (Donated by Protestant Chaplain, Randolph AFB, Texas)

This Protestant cross was used at Randolph Air Force Base, Texas, from 1936 to 1972.

189

The explosion of this Russian-made rocket destroyed the U.S. Air Force chapel at Ton Son Nhut Air Base, Vietnam, on February 18, 1968.

An American POW sketched this chapel in the hospital area of the World War II Japanese prison camp at Cabanatuan, the Philippines.

190

9 Behind the Scenes

There's more to the Air Force Museum than what is on display for viewing by the general public. A great deal of activity goes on behind the scenes to acquire and prepare airplanes and other items for display. Much work transpires within the museum's administrative offices.

A great deal more goes on across the airfield in World War II hangars that are commonly referred to as the restoration area. The remainder of Wright Field is not open to the public because of safety considerations, but the restoration area is open to museum visitors on a limited, controlled basis on Friday afternoons in the summer.

Visitors with a scholarly or professional interest, however, are eligible to use the archives of the museum's research division. It is located on the second floor of the museum and is operated by several people who provide historical data in support of the museum's acquisition, restoration, exhibits, and public information functions. The staffs work with more than two hundred thousand documents, including technical manuals, test reports, books, periodicals, drawings, photographs, films, video tapes, and other material dealing with the history of aviation and the Air Force. Most of the material was obtained from military agencies or as donations from civilian sources.

Museum staff members use this data in a variety of ways. They attempt to determine what artifacts are lacking but necessary to tell the Air Force story. Then they attempt to locate those items. Information in the research division also provides guidance as to how old aircraft should be refurbished or how mannequins should be uniformed. In addition, the research people are responsible for carefully researching and writing much of the explanatory material that appears throughout the museum's exhibit area. Of course, they work closely with the museum director, curator, and collections management, exhibits, and restoration staffs to ensure that the exhibits are authentic, informative and attractive.

Among qualified researchers and aviation enthusiasts who have visited the museum and performed their own research are authors, historians, patent attorneys, engineers, students, model builders, and artists. The research division is open on weekdays from 9:00 A.M. to 4:00 P.M. Personal assistance from staff members is dependent upon their current workload, the subject matter, and the significance of the research project.

The museum curator has an office on the second floor of the museum where he determines what is to be displayed and prepares necessary historical data. His selections are coordinated with the director and converted into displays by the exhibits division. Finished products may include restored aircraft brought to the museum in pieces from a crash site or barn, a copy of an extinct airplane built from original plans, early flying machines and costumed figures in a diorama window, or a collection of historical artifacts and enlarged photographs mounted on wallboards. Often, when preparing airplanes or missiles for display, the restoration staff must manufacture its own spare parts. The replacement part is always authentic, built from original specifications by museum employees and volunteers who work together in the restoration hangars.

From time to time a fully restored aircraft is presented to the museum ready for display. For instance, the 133rd Tactical Airlift Wing of the Minnesota Air National Guard restored a P-35 which the museum received in mid-1974. It is the last known remaining P-35. This type of aircraft was the first single-seat, all-metal pursuit airplane with retractable landing gear and enclosed cockpit in regular service with the Air Corps. Room was quickly made for it in the museum.

In addition to the approximately six thousand items on exhibit at the museum, there are some twenty-three thousand others on loan to four hundred other museums and display sites. Fifteen thousand items are stored by the collections management division in the restoration area. The collection there includes aircraft, uniform clothing, parachutes, engines, armament, art, aircraft instruments, propellers, missiles, prisoner-of-war memorabilia, aerial photographic equipment, communications gear, space items, flags, insignia, decorations, trophies, and more. All are available for use by the museum or for other official purposes.

Ample free parking is available for visitors to the museum. Oftentimes they may view aircraft directly overhead on their final approach for landing at nearby Patterson Field (Areas A and C).

Three volunteer tour guides are briefed on the arrangement of aircraft at the museum. The tours are conducted during the school year and must be scheduled in advance. *U.S. Air Force photo.*

Museum researchers spend a great deal of time searching through their records to verify that the exhibits being planned will be accurate and authentic.

Construction plans for the Sopwith Camel and many other airplanes are on file at the museum. The research division periodically reviews such plans for its own staff and for the general public.

More than 75,000 documents dealing mainly with military aviation are on file at the museum. Only a portion is stored here.

A father and his sons with an interest in the B-29 look through research division files as they pursue their hobby. Aviation writers and patent attorneys, among others, have used this service. An appointment is required.

When research division staffers learned that an individual was planning to donate a Vultee L-5 to the museum, they began looking for information on how these liaison airplanes were painted in World War II. An old *Air Force Magazine* article on L-5s in New Guinea put them on the trail of James D. Nichols, who flew L-5s as a technical sergeant in the wilds of New Guinea some thirty years before. After numerous telephone calls, they found him with the California Air National Guard. Nichols provided the needed information, complete with the following snapshots, which the museum has copied. The Vultee L-5 now exhibited in the museum appears with the markings of the so-called Guinea Short Lines of World War II. Tech. Sgt. James D. Nichols poses in front of the operations hut of the 25th Liaison Squadron Detachment at Sentini Air Strip, Hollandia, West New Guinea.

Guinea Short Lines pilots who rescued downed crews, strafed Japanese emplacements, and led fighters to concealed jungle targets.

The L-5s seldom used improved airstrips. Here the plane attracts the attention of Papuan natives.

Two or three stretcher patients could be carried by the L-5 for rapid delivery to an awaiting ambulance of the Guinea Short Lines.

Retired Lt. Col. Iceal E. "Gene" Hambleton *(right)* is also known as "Bat 21", immortalized during the 1980s in a book and movie by the same name. In 1990 he donated his flight suit, rescue radio, cap, and other items to the museum before a public lecture. Accepting them are Curator Jack B. Hilliard and Director Richard L. Uppstom, who holds the radio which Colonel Hambleton used during his 11½ days successfully eluding North Vietnam soldiers. *U.S. Air Force photo.*

When lettering on historic documents or artifacts fade and is no longer visible to the naked eye, museum photographer Harry Elliott uses modern technology to retrieve the lost information. For instance, an infrared-barrier filter can be placed on the lens of a video camera *(top, center)*. If an image can then be seen on the monitor *(right)*, infrared film in a standard camera can produce an image to be printed on photographic paper. Such a procedure retrieved the signatures that had "disappeared" from the souvenir Japanese flag *(below)* from World War II. *Springfield News-Sun photo.*

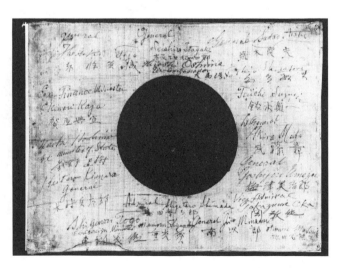

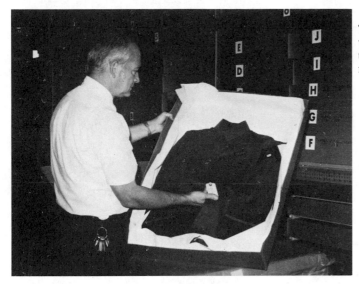

This World War I uniform of the Air Service is wrapped in acid barrier paper to prevent the acid in the cardboard box from deteriorating the vintage garment.

Individual record cards are maintained by the collections management division on each of the museum's 44,000-plus items. This card is for an inverted Liberty engine the museum obtained in December 1948.

While recuperating in a convent hospital during World War I, a downed American pilot made this flag for his French hosts. When restored it will be displayed under special plexiglas that will filter damaging ultraviolet rays.

Small items such as aircraft instruments and parts are stored in bins for future use on restored aircraft or in displays of their own.

A propeller hub on President Eisenhower's aircraft is polished prior to returning it to public display. Openings in the engine have been covered with plexiglas to keep out birds.

Placement of display items is carefully worked out by the exhibits division long before an exhibit is moved across the field to the museum. The candy-striped plane is a model of the Spad 13 flown in World War I by Capt. Reed Chambers, who succeeded Capt. Eddie Rickenbacker as commander of the 94th Aero Squadron.

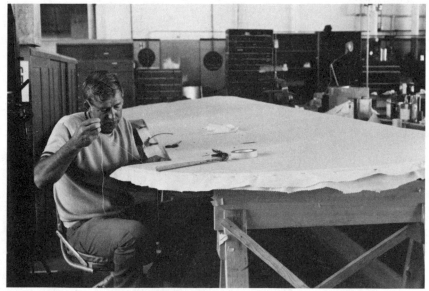

Meticulous sewing is only part of the work involved in restoring the wings of an O-38 which rested in the wilds of Alaska for about thirty years.

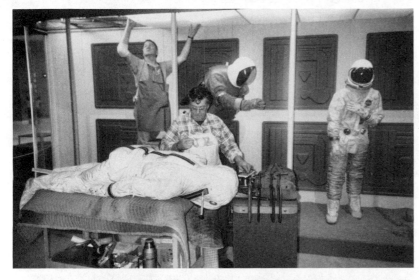

Much of the work for the enlarged and upgraded Space Gallery was done in 1989-90 behind the scenes in Hangar 4. Then the new exhibits, such as this one dealing with space suits, were reassembled by exhibits division personnel at the museum.

Volunteers perform a variety of important tasks, including the manufacture of replacement parts for aircraft being restored. Several hundred men and women donate their time and talents to assist throughout the museum. *U.S. Air Force photo.*

All of the old Irish linen and thousands of rusty, small nails had to be removed from the wings of the Caproni bomber during its restoration. That and much more had to be done to its fuselage. Two pilots *(seated with their backs to the fuel tanks)* and two other crew members routinely flew over the Alps in this open-cockpit bi-plane. The Ca.36 came to the U.S. Air Force Museum from Italy in 1987 in fourteen crates aboard a USAF transport. *U.S. Air Force photo.*

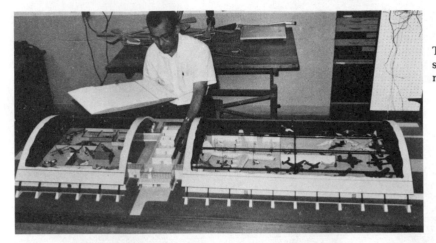

Three-dimensional models are used to better visualize the arrangement of displays within the museum.

Refurbishing heavy steel beams and manufacturing new parts are part of the process in getting this Bomarc missile ready for display.

Starting with a few original pieces, museum craftsmen have built a Sopwith Camel of World War I fame. It includes a wicker seat made by museum workers from original drawings.

Not all museum aircraft are on display at all times, as some are being restored and others are awaiting restoration. When this photograph was taken, President Eisenhower's VC-121E *Columbine* (*right*) was nearly ready to be returned to its position in front of the museum. Work was continuing on the Bell P-39Q *Airacobra,* which made its first flight in 1939 at Wright Field. Nearly 4,800 were allotted to the Russians during World War II.

This portion of the Air Force Museum was dedicated in 1976 with actor James Stewart as the master of ceremonies and Senator Barry M. Goldwater as the keynote speaker. Both flew for the Army Air Force in World War II. A large amount of the approximately $900,000 addition came from the estate of Brig. Gen. Erik H. Nelson, who died in 1970. He was a participant in 1924 in the first flight around the world.

The original "airfoil" roof is visible where the 1976 addition joins the 1971 structure. Secretary of the Air Force Thomas C. Reed cut the ribbon for the 1976 ceremony with a pair of scissors once used by Orville Wright.

From the second floor gallery, a portion of the two-story addition is seen on the right. A restaurant occupies the top floor while a reception area, gift shop, bookstore, and tour guide office occupy the first floor. Offices of the Air Force Museum Foundation, Inc., and a conference room are on the mezzanine.

Appendix

All Department of Defense aircraft have been assigned designations to conform with joint Army-Navy-Air Force regulations.

Each aircraft or missile system designation has one letter to denote its primary function or capability; e.g., "B" for bomber, "F" for fighter, etc. To this, one or more prefixes are added to denote modified mission and status for aircraft, or mission and launch environment for missiles.

For example, in the designation VC-137, the basic mission or type is "C," cargo/transport. The "V" prefix denotes the modified mission of transporting staff personnel. If the designation were YVC-137, the additional "Y" prefix would denote prototype status. Suffixes are also used with aircraft designations to denote different models of the basic aircraft. Thus, the C-137B would be a newer version of the C-137A.

The following prefixes have been used for many years although not all apply to USAF aircraft.

In a missile system example, one model of the Minuteman ICBM is the LGM-30G. In this case, the vehicle type is "M" for guided missile. The prefix "G" denotes the mission, surface attack, and the additional prefix "L" gives the launch environment, silo-launched. If this LGM designation was prefixed with an "X," it would mean the missile system's status was experimental.

Status Prefix Symbols

AEROSPACE VEHICLES

Letter	Title	Description
G[1]	Permanently Grounded	Aircraft permanently grounded and utilized for ground instruction and training.
J	Special Test, Temporary	Aerospace vehicles on special test programs by authorized organizations, or on bailment contract, having a special test configuration, or whose installed property has been temporarily removed to accommodate the test.
N	Special Test, Permanent	Aerospace vehicles on special test programs by authorized activities, or on bailment contract, whose configuration is so drastically changed that return to its original configuration or conversion to standard operational configuration is beyond practicable or economic limits.
X	Experimental	Aerospace vehicles in a development, experimental stage where the basic mission symbol and design number have been designated, but not established as a standard vehicle for service use.
Y	Prototype	Aerospace vehicles procured in limited quantities, usually prior to production decision, to serve as models or patterns.
Z	Planning	Aerospace vehicles in the planning or predevelopment stage.

Modified Mission Symbols

AIRCRAFT

A	Attack	Aircraft modified to search out, attack, and destroy enemy land or sea targets, using conventional or special weapons. This symbol also describes aircraft used for interdiction and close air support missions.
C	Cargo/Transport	Aircraft modified for carrying cargo/passengers or medical patients.
D	Director	Aircraft modified for controlling drone aircraft or a missile.
E	Special Electronic Installation	Aircraft modified with electronic devices for employment in one or more of the following missions: (1) Electronic countermeasures. (2) Airborne early warning radar. (3) Airborne command and control, including communications relay. (4) Tactical data communications link for all nonautonomous modes of flight.

[1]Applies only to aircraft.

Letter	Title	Description
H	Search Rescue	Aircraft modified and equipped for performance of search and rescue missions.
K	Tanker	Aircraft modified and equipped to provide in-flight refueling of other aircraft.
L	Cold Weather	Aircraft modified for operation in the Arctic and Antarctic regions; includes skis, special insulation, and other ancillary equipment required for extreme cold weather operations.
M	Mine Countermeasures	Aircraft modified for aerial mine countermeasures and minesweeping missions.
O	Observation	Aircraft modified to observe (through visual or other means) and report tactical information concerning composition and disposition of enemy forces, troops, and supplies in an active combat area.
P	Patrol	Long-range, all-weather, multi-engine aircraft operating from land and/or water bases, modified for independent accomplishment of: antisubmarine warfare; maritime reconnaissance; and mining function.
Q	Drone	Aircraft modified to be controlled from a point outside the aircraft.
R	Reconnaissance	Aircraft modified and permanently equipped for photographic and/or electronic reconnaissance missions.
S	Antisubmarine	Aircraft modified so that it can function to search, identify, attack, and destroy enemy submarines.
T	Trainer	Aircraft modified and equipped for training purposes.
U	Utility	Aircraft, having small payload, modified to perform miscellaneous missions, such as carrying cargo or passengers, towing targets, etc.
V	Staff	Aircraft modified to provide accommodations, such as chairs, tables, lounge, berths, etc., for the transportation of staff personnel.
W	Weather	Aircraft modified and equipped for meteorological missions.

Launch Environment Symbols

ROCKETS AND GUIDED MISSILES

A	Air	Vehicles air launched.
B	Multiple	Vehicles capable of being launched from more than one environment.

Letter	*Title*	*Description*
C	Coffin	Vehicles stored horizontally or at less than a 45-degree angle in a protective enclosure (regardless of structural strength) and launched from the ground.
F	Individual	Vehicles carried and launched by one individual.
G	Runway	Vehicles launched from a runway.
H	Silo-Stored	Vehicles vertically stored below ground level and launched from the ground.
L	Silo-Launched	Vehicles vertically stored and launched from below ground level.
M	Mobile	Vehicles launched from a ground vehicle or movable platform.
P	Soft Pad	Vehicles partially or nonprotected in storage and launched from the ground.
R	Ship	Vehicles launched from a surface vessel—such as ship, barge, etc.
U	Underwater	Vehicles launched from a submarine or other underwater device.

Basic Mission and Type Symbols

AIRCRAFT

A	Attack	Aircraft designed to search out, attack, and destroy enemy land or sea targets, using conventional or special weapons. This symbol also applies to aircraft used for interdiction and close air support missions.
B	Bomber	Aircraft designed for bombing enemy targets.
C	Cargo/Transport	Aircraft designed for carrying cargo/passengers or medical patients.
E	Special Electronic Installation	Aircraft equipped with electronic devices for employment in one or more of the following missions: (1) Electronic countermeasures. (2) Airborne early warning radar. (3) Airborne command and control, including communications relay. (4) Tactical data communications link for all nonautonomous modes of flight.
F	Fighter	Aircraft designed to intercept and destroy other aircraft and/or missiles (includes multi-purpose aircraft also designed for ground support missions); for example, interdiction and close air support.
H[2]	Helicopter	Rotary-wing aircraft designed with the capability of flight in any plane; for example, horizontal, vertical, or diagonal.

---

[2] Type Symbols.

Letter	*Title*	*Description*
K	Tanker	Aircraft designed for in-flight refueling of other aircraft.
O	Observation	Aircraft designed to observe (through visual or other means) and report tactical information concerning composition and disposition of enemy forces, troops, and supplies in an active combat area.
P	Patrol	Long-range, all-weather, multi-engine aircraft operating from land and/or water bases, designed for independent accomplishment of: antisubmarine warfare; maritime reconnaissance; and mining function.
R	Reconnaissance	Aircraft designed to perform reconnaissance missions.
S	Antisubmarine	Aircraft designed to search out, detect, identify, attack, and destroy enemy submarines.
T	Trainer	Aircraft designed for training personnel in the operation of aircraft and/or related equipment, and having provisions for instructor personnel.
U	Utility	Aircraft designed for miscellaneous missions, such as carrying cargo and/or passengers, towing targets, etc. These aircraft will include those having a small payload.
V[2]	VTOL and STOL	Aircraft designed for vertical takeoff or landing with no takeoff or landing roll, or aircraft capable of takeoff and landing in a minimum prescribed distance.
X	Research	Aircraft designed for testing configurations of a radical nature. These aircraft are not normally intended for use as tactical aircraft.

Mission Symbols

ROCKETS AND GUIDED MISSILES

D	Decoy	Vehicles designed or modified to confuse, deceive, or divert enemy defenses by simulating an attack vehicle.

---

[2]Type Symbols.

Letter	Title	Description
E	Special Electronic	Vehicles designed or modified with electronic equipment for communications, countermeasures, electronic radiation sounding, or other electronic recording or relay missions.
G	Surface Attack	Vehicles designed to destroy enemy land or sea targets.
I	Intercept-Aerial	Vehicles designed to intercept aerial targets in defensive or offensive roles.
Q	Drone	Vehicles designed for target, reconnaissance, or surveillance purposes.
T	Training	Vehicles designed or permanently modified for training purposes.
U	Underwater Attack	Vehicles designed to destroy enemy submarines or other underwater targets, or to detonate underwater.
W	Weather	Vehicles designed to observe, record, or relay data pertaining to meteorological phenomena.

Type Symbols

ROCKETS AND GUIDED MISSILES

M	Guided Missile	Unmanned, self-propelled vehicles designed to move in a trajectory or flight path all or partially above the earth's surface, and whose trajectory or course, while the vehicle is in motion, is capable of being controlled remotely or by homing systems, or by inertial and/or programmed guidance from within. This term does not include space vehicles, space launch vehicles (space boosters), or naval torpedoes, but it does include target and reconnaissance drones.
N	Probe	Nonorbital instrumented vehicles (not involved in space missions) that are used to penetrate the aerospace environment and transmit or report back information.
R	Rocket	Self-propelled vehicles, without installed or remote control guidance mechanisms, whose trajectory or flight path cannot be altered after launch. Normally, rocket systems designed for line-of-sight ground fire against ground targets are not included.

INVENTORY

AIRCRAFT, MISSILES, AND SPACECRAFT
UNITED STATES AIR FORCE MUSEUM
Wright-Patterson Air Force Base, Ohio

Explanation of Inventory Codes.

STATUS CODES

A   Active; still being flown on occasion.

C   Under Active Restoration; location given if not at W-PAFB.

D   Derelict Wreckage or Severely Damaged; may be restored or used for parts.

PV   On Public View; readily available in the exhibit buildings or the Air Park.

RA   Research Accessible; for serious researchers, with prior permission.

S   Stored; not accessible for viewing.

X   Displayed in markings not used on this particular aircraft when active.

LOCATION CODES

A   Annex; Hanger 1 or 9

AP   Outdoor Air Park; adjacent to the main exhibit buildings.

APC   Air Power Gallery; north section of front exhibit building.

EYG   Early Years Gallery; south section of front exhibit building.

HH   Hall of Honor; center core of front building.

MFG   Modern Flight Gallery; second exhibit building.

MP   Outdoor Missile Park; in front of main exhibit buildings.

R   Restoration; Hangar 4C or 4D.

RR   Outdoor Restoration Ramp; in front of Hangars 4C, D & E.

S   Storage; Hangar 1 or 4E

SG   Space Gallery; portion of north section of front exhibit building.

*   Suspended at this location.

Aircraft or Missle	Status	Location
Aerojet Aerobee Rocket	PV	SG
Aeronca L–3B Grasshopper	PV	APG*
American Helicopter XH–26 Jet Jeep	RA	S
Beechcraft VC–6A	PV	A
Beech UC–43 Traveller	PVX	EYG
Beech C–45H Expeditor	PV	A
Beech AT–10	D	S
Beech AT–10	D	S
Beech AT–11 Kansan	PVX	EYG
Beechcraft T–34A Mentor	PV	MFG
Bell P–39Q Airacobra	PVX	APG
Bell P–59B Airacomet	PV	APG
Bell P–63E King Cobra	PV	A
Bell UH–1P Iroquois	PV	MFG*
Bell UH–13J	PV	A
Bell X–1B	PV	MFG
Bell X–5	RA	S
Bell XGAM (XB–63) Rascal	PV	MFG
Benson X–25A Gyrocopter	PV	APG*
Bleriot 1911	PV	EYG*
Bristol Beaufighter	C	Colo.
Boeing AGM–69 Short Range Attack Missile	PV	MFG
Boeing AGM–86B Air-Launched Cruise Missile	PV	MFG*
Boeing B–17G Flying Fortress	PV	APG
Boeing B–29 Superfortress	PV	APG
Boeing B–29 Walk-Through Fuselage	PV	APG
Boeing B–47E Stratojet	PVX	MFG
Boeing WB–50D Superfortress	PV	AP
Boeing KB–50J Superfortress	PVX	AP
Boeing B–52D Stratofortress	PV	MFG
Boeing KC–97L Stratofreighter	PV	AP
Boeing CIM–10A Bomarc Missile	PV	MP
Boeing NKC–135A Stratotanker	PV	AP
Boeing LGM–30A Minuteman I	PV	MP
Boeing LGM–30G Minuteman II	PV	MP
Boeing P–12E	PV	EYG
Boeing Stearman PT–13D Kaydet	PV	EYG
Boeing PT–17	A	R
Boeing YQM–94A Compass Cope	PV	A
Caproni Ca–36	PV	EYG
Caquot Type R Observation Balloon	PV	EYG
CASA 2.111H (He–111H)	RA	S
CASA 352L (Ju 52)+	PVX	AP
Cessna YA–37A Dragonfly	PV	APG
Cessna UC–78B Bobcat	PV	MFG*
Cessna 0–1G Bird Dog	PV	APG*
Cessna 0–2A Skymaster	PV	APG*
Cessna T–37B	PV	MFG*
Cessna U–3A	PV	MFG*
Chanute 1904 Glider Reproduction	PV	HH
Chrysler PGM–19 Jupiter Missile	PV	MP
Consolidated B–24D Liberator	PV	APG
Consolidated PBY–5A Catalina (OA–10A)+	PVX	MFG
Consolidated PT–1 Trusty	PV	EYG*

Aircraft or Missle	Status	Location
Convair B–36J	PV	APG
Convair B–58A Hustler	PV	MFG
Convair C–131D	PV	A
Convair XF–92A	R	R/Bldg. 13
Convair F–102A Delta Dagger	PV	APG
Convair F–106A Delta Dart	PV	MFG
Convair HGM–16F Atlas Missile	RA	RR
Culver PQ–14B Drone	PV	A
Curtiss C–46D Commando	PVX	MFG
Curtiss 1911 "D" Reproduction	PV	EYG
Curtiss JN–4D Jenny	PV	EYG
Curtiss O–52 Owl	PVX	MFG*
Curtiss P–6E Hawk	PVX	EYG
Curtiss P–36A Hawk	PVX	EYG
Curtiss P–40E Kittyhawk	PVX	EYG
Curtiss–Wright AT–9 Fledgling	PV	MFG
Curtiss–Wright AT–9 Fledging	D	S
Dart Aerial Gunnery Target	PV	APG*
DeHavilland DH–4	PVX	EYG
DeHavilland DH–89 Dominie (Dragon Rapide)+	PVX	A
DeHavilland DH–98 Mosquito B.35	PVX	APG
DeHavilland Canada C–7A Caribou	PV	AP
DeHavilland Canada U–6A Beaver	PVX	MFG*
Douglas A–1E Skyraider	PV	APG
Douglas A–20G Havoc	PVX	MFG
Douglas A–26A Counter-Invader (B–26K)+	PV	A
Douglas A–26C Invader	PVX	APG
Douglas B–18A Bolo	PVX	MFG
Douglas B–23 Dragon	PVX	AP
Douglas RB–66B Destroyer	PV	MFG
Douglas C–39A	PVX	A
Douglas C–47D Skytrain	PVX	MFG
Douglas C–53C Skytrooper	RA	RR
Douglas VC–54C Skymaster	C	R
Douglas VC–118 Liftmaster	PV	A
Douglas C–124C Globemaster II	PVX	MFG
Douglas C–133A Cargo Master	PV	AP
Douglas O–38F	PV	EYG
Douglas O–46A	PVX	MFG*
Douglas PGM–17 Thor Missile	PV	MP
Douglas X–3 Stilleto	PVX	MFG
Fairchild C–82A Packet	PVX	AP
Fairchild XUC–86A Forwarder	RA	S
Fairchild C–119J Flying Boxcar	PV	AP
Fairchild C–123K Provider	PV	AP
Fairchild PT–19 Cornell	PVX	EYG
Fairchild PT–26 Cornell	PVX	A
Fairchild Republic A–10A Thunderbolt II	PVX	AP
Fieseler Fi 156 Storch	PV	APG*
Fisher P–75A Eagle	PV	A
Focke–Achgelis FA–330A–1 Bachstelze	PV	EYG*
Focke–Wulf Fw 190D–9	PV	APG
Fokker D–VII	S	S
Fokker DR–1	S	S

+Displayed as indicated within parentheses.

Aircraft or Missile	Status	Location	Aircraft or Missile	Status	Location
Ford JB–2 (V–1 Buzz Bomb)+	PV	APG	McDonnell F–101B Voodoo	PV	A
General Dynamics F–111A	PV	MFG	McDonnell RF–101C Voodoo	PV	MFG
Grumman J2F–6 Duck (OA–12)+	PVX	MFG	McDonnell Quail Decoy Missile	PV	MFG
Grumman HU–16B Albatross	PV	MFG	McDonnell XH–20	PV	APG*
Halberstadt CL IV	R	Berlin	McDonnell Mercury Spacecraft	PV	SG
Hawker Hurricane Mk. IIa	PV	EYG	McDonnell Gemini Spacecraft	PV	SG
Hawker VX–6A (P.1127) Kestrel	PV	A	Messerschmitt Me 262A Schwalbe	PV	APG
Helio U–10D Super Courier	PVX	MFG*	Mikoyan–Gurevich MiG–15 Fagot	PV	APG
Hispano HA.1112K (Me–109G)+	PVX	APG	Mikoyan–Gurevich MiG–17 Fresco	PVX	MFG
Interstate L–6	RA	S	Mikoyan–Gurevich MiG–21F		
Junkers Ju 88D–1	PV	A	Fishbed–C	PVX	MFG
Kaman HH–43B Huskie	PV	MFG*	Mitsubishi A6M2 Zero Sen	C	Okla.
Kawanishi NIK2–J Shinden Kai			Nieuport 28	PVX	EYG
(George 21)	PVX	APG	Noorduyn UC–64A Norseman	PVX	APG*
Kettering Aerial Torpedo Reproduction	PV	EYG*	North American A–36A Apache	PVX	MFG
Kugisho MXY–7K1 Ohka II			North American B–25D Mitchell		
Suicide Bomb	PV	APG*	(B–25B)+	PVX	APG
Laister–Kaufman TG–4A	RA	S	North American B–45C Tornado	PVX	MFG
Link Trainer (Model C–3)	PV	EYG	North American XB–70 Valkyrie	PV	MFG
LTV A–7D Corsair II	PVX	MFG	North American F–82B Twin Mustang	PV	APG
LTV XC–142A	PV	A	North American F–86A Sabre	PVX	APG
Lockheed C–60A Lodestar	PV	A	North American F–86D Sabre	PVX	MFG
Lockheed VC–121E Constellation	PV	A	North American F–86H Sabre		
Lockheed EC–121D Constellation	PV	AP	(Skinless)	PV	APG
Lockheed JC–130A Hercules			North American F–100C Super Sabre	PV	APG
(AC–130A)+	PV	A	North American F–100D Super Sabre	PV	MFG
Lockheed VC–140B Jet Star	PV	A	North American F–107A	PV	A
Lockheed YF–12A Black Frog	PV	A	North American O–47B	PVX	A
Lockheed SR–71 Blackbird	PV	MFG	North American P–51D Mustang	PVX	APG
Lockheed F–80C Shooting Star	PV	APG	North Amcrican T–6G Texan (AT–6G)+	PVX	EYG
Lockheed F–94A Starfire	PV	APG	North American T–6G Texan	AX	WP–
Lockheed F–94C Starfire	PVX	MFG			AFB
Lockheed F–104A Starfighter	PV	Front	North American BT–14		
Lockheed F–104C Starfighter	PV	MFG	(NA–64/YALE I)	PVX	EYG*
Lockheed F–117A Stealth	PV	MFG	North American T–28A Trojan	PV	MFG
Lockheed P–38L Lightning	PVX	APG	North American T–28B Trojan	PV	A
Lockheed P–80R Shooting Star	PV	APG	North American T–39A Sabreliner	PV	A
Lockheed T–33A Shooting Star	PV	APG	North American X–10 Navajo		
Lockheed U–2A	PV	MFG*	Test Vehicle	PV	A
Lockheed X–17 Research Rocket	PV	MFG	North American X–15A	PV	MFG
Loening OA–1A	PV	EYG	North American AGM–28 Hound		
Martin B–10	PVX	EYG	Dog Missile	PV	MFG
Martin B–26G Marauder	PVX	APG	North American Rockwell Apollo 15		
Martin CGM–13B Mace Missile	PV	MP	Command Module	PV	SG
Martin EB–57B Canberra	PV	MFG	Northrop A–17A	RA	S
Martin HGM–25A Titan I Missile	PV	MP	Northrop YF–5A Freedom Fighter	PV	MFG
Martin SV–5J (X–24A)+	PVX	SG	Northrop F–89J Scorpion	PVX	MFG
Martin SV–5D Lifting Body	PV	SG	Northrop P–61C Black Widow		
Martin TM–61A Matador Missile	PV	MP	(P–61B)+	PVX	APG
Martin X–24B	PV	MFG	Northrop SM–62 Snark Missile	PV	MP
McDonnell ASV–3 Lifting Body	PV	SG	Northrop T–38A Talon	PV	MFG
McDonnell–Douglas F–4C Phantom II	PV	MFG	Northrop X–4 Bantam	PV	MFG*
McDonnell–Douglas YF–4E Phantom II	PV	A	Packard LePere LUSAC–11	C	R
McDonnell–Douglas F–4 "Call to Glory"			Piper L–4 Grasshopper	PV	EYG*
Fuselage	PV	MFG	Piper PA–48 Enforcer	RA	S
McDonnell–Douglas F–15A Eagle	PVX	AP	Pratt–Read TG–32 (LNE–1)	RA	S
McDonnell XF–85 Goblin	PV	APG	Radioplane OQ–2A Target Drone	PV	EYG*

+Displayed as indicated within parentheses.

Aircraft or Missle	Status	Location	Aircraft or Missle	Status	Location
Radioplane OQ–19 Target Drone	PV	APG	Sikorsky R–4B Hoverfly	PV	APG*
Republic F–84E Thunderjet	PV	APG	Sikorsky R–6A Hoverfly II	PVX	APG*
Republic F–84F Thunderstreak	PV	APG	Sopwith Camel Reproduction	PV	EYG
Republic YRF–84F Thunderstreak	PV	A	Soviet SA–2 Surface–to–Air Missile	PV	APG
Republic RF–84K	RA	RR	SPAD VII	PVX	EYG
Republic XF–91 Thunderceptor	PV	A	SPAD XVI	PV	EYG
Republic F–105B Thunderchief	PV	AP	Sperry–Verville M–1 Messenger	PVX	EYG*
Republic F–105D Thunderchief	C	R	Standard J–1 Airplane	PVX	EYG*
Republic F–105G Thunderchief	PV	MFG	Standard J–1 Airplane (Skinless)	PV	EYG*
Republic P–47D Thunderbolt	PVX	APG	Stinson L–5 Sentinel	PVX	APG*
Republic P–47D Thunderbolt	PVX	A	Supermarine Spitfire PR.XI	C	Colo.
Rockwell International B–1A Lancer	PV	AP	Supermarine Spitfire LF.XVIe	PVX	A
Royal Aircraft Factory (Eberhardt)			Taylorcraft L–2M Grasshopper	PVX	APG*
SE–5E	PV	EYG	Teledyne Ryan AQM–34L Firebee		
Ryan BQM–34 Firebee Drone	PV	MFG*	Drone	PV	MFG
Ryan L–17A Navion	PVX	A	Thomas–Morse S4C Scout	PV	EYG*
Ryan PT–22 Recruit	PVX	EYG	Vertol CH–21A Workhorse	PV	A
Ryan ST–A (YPT–16)+	PVX	EYG	Vultee L–1A Vigilant	PV	APG*
Ryan X–13 Vertijet	PV	MFG	Vultee BT–13B Valiant	PV	EYG
Schweizer TG–3A Training Glider	PV	EYG*	WACO CG–4A Hadrian Glider	PVX	APG
Seversky P–35A	PV	EYG	Westland Lysander MkIII	PVX	A
Sikorsky CH–3E	RA	RR	Wright 1909 Military Flyer		
Sikorsky CH–3E Black Maria	PV	AP	Reproduction	PV	EYG
Sikorsky YH–5A	PV	MFG	Wright 1911 Modified B Flyer	PV	EYG
Sikorsky UH–19B Chickasaw	PVX	APG			

+Displayed as indicated within parentheses.

It took a bit of planning to move this Boeing B-52D into the Modern Flight Gallery. Museum staffers succeeded by turning its landing gear at an angle and towing the Stratofortress indoors sideways. They also dropped the hinged tail. Other museum facilities are visible in the background: double-hangar Annex *(left of center)* and Hanger 4 *(far right)*, home of the collections management, restoration, and exhibits divisions. *U.S. Air Force photo.*

Index

Italic page numbers indicate illustrations

More than 20,000 spectators witnessed the last USAF landing of a Lockheed SR-71 when this Blackbird touched down in March 1990 on the runway at the south end of the main museum complex. The U.S. Air Force Museum also owns the SR-71s displayed at other museums around the country. *U.S. Air Force photo by Brian Barr.*